PRAISE FOR

COACH WOODEN
ONE-ON-ONE

John Wooden has been steady as a rock because he's been grounded
on the Rock. We have known that but haven't known much about it.
His life as a coach and as a man has influenced me greatly. His faith,
expressed in this book, has now led me closer to God. Thank you, Coach,
for impacting my life and for completing your legacy.

Jerry Colangelo
MANAGING GENERAL PARTNER, ARIZONA DIAMONDBACKS
CHAIRMAN, CEO AND MANAGING GENERAL PARTNER, PHOENIX SUNS

If we want to win in basketball, we have to know the fundamentals.
The same is true in life. John Wooden has been a winner both on and
off the court. He knows the game plan. In *Coach Wooden: One-on-One*,
he lays out the plan in a way that anyone can follow—starting with
the fundamental principles. Each page offers a challenge
that will help you be a winner at life.

Denny Crum
FORMER HEAD COACH, MEN'S BASKETBALL
UNIVERSITY OF LOUISVILLE

What comes to mind when I think of Coach Wooden,
whom I call Papa, is his continual kindness and unselfishness
toward others, demonstrated through his actions and words.
Papa has a gift for making people think about how important
the Lord is in their lives, how we should love one another
and how full life is with Jesus in it.

Ann Meyers Drysdale
UCLA CLASS OF '78
WOMEN'S BASKETBALL HALL OF FAMER AND TELEVISION BROADCASTER

I watched Coach Wooden from afar and have tremendous respect for what he has accomplished. Coach Wooden has a commonsense approach to everyday life. Even if you are not an athlete, you'll gain a great deal from his lessons.

Joe Gibbs
FORMER HEAD COACH
WASHINGTON REDSKINS

I have looked up to John Wooden in his roles as a coach, as a man and as a Christian. His example as a coach has deeply influenced the way I coach. His example as a man has been a pleasure to see—strength coupled with sensitivity, instead of macho. His example as a Christian demonstrates faith in action. In *Coach Wooden: One-on-One* we see all three combined in very practical ways. Thank you, Coach, for putting it all together for us.

Sylvia Hatchell
HEAD WOMEN'S BASKETBALL COACH
UNIVERSITY OF NORTH CAROLINA
1994 NATIONAL CHAMPIONS

I've always felt disheartened to read about athletes or celebrities who thank their lucky stars for their successes. Coach Wooden thanks God for the life he has lived, and I believe that his faith and humility have been a major part of his success. These qualities serve as examples to all of us.

C. J. Hobgood
PROFESSIONAL SURFER, 2001 WORLD CHAMPION

John Wooden is an icon who has spent his 92 years desiring to represent God through his walk. His coaching expertise and philosophy for living life are well known. Now my friend Jay Carty has helped us to get a glimpse of Coach's spiritual side. It's a side worth seeing.

Tim LaHaye
AUTHOR, LEFT BEHIND SERIES

My favorite quote by Coach Wooden is "Be more concerned with your character than with your reputation, because your character is what you really are, while your reputation is merely what others think pyou are." The definition of integrity is lining up who you are with who others think you are. Coach Wooden is one of the rare men of our times with seamless integrity. This book explores the anchor points in Coach's life that enabled him to stand tall when others fell so easily. His unquestionable character serves as an example to us all.

Steve Largent
FORMER CONGRESSMAN, AND NFL HALL OF FAMER

The combo of Coach Wooden and Jay Carty is as good as Stockton and Malone, Mantle and Maris, hotdogs and mustard, and March and madness. You can bet this book will generate lots of points with lots of folks.

Max Lucado
AUTHOR AND PULPIT MINISTER
OAK HILLS CHURCH OF CHRIST
SAN ANTONIO, TEXAS

Coach Wooden is a legend all around the world, and he has influenced everyone who plays the game. His teachings, his championships and, most important, his integrity serve as a legacy to millions of basketball players and fans for generations to come. Thank you, Coach Wooden, for all you have done for this great game!

Yao Ming
HOUSTON ROCKETS

As a UCLA basketball player, I had the privilege of watching John Wooden every day of the basketball season for three years. Because of his impeccable example, he became somewhat of a living devotional for me. Without an abundance of spoken words, John Wooden lived a life committed to biblical principles, day in and day out. Now Jay Carty and John Wooden have created a devotional that has taken my mentor's Christlike deeds and put them into words so that all of us can share in the wisdom.

Swen Nater
FORMER UCLA AND NBA PLAYER
COSTCO ASSISTANT BUYER, SPORTING GOODS

As iron sharpens iron,
God's wisdom to unfold
merged His two entrusted vessels
to harvest His pearls of gold.

Coach Wooden and Jay Carty have conferred with
each other, and from the foundry of their experiences, we have
a book of pure, life-changing nuggets.

Willie Naulls
UCLA ALL-AMERICAN, AND FOUR-TIME NBA ALL-STAR
THREE-TIME WORLD CHAMPION, BOSTON CELTICS

John Wooden is a legend who is also a gentleman. He has represented
Christ well over the years. Other books have told us about his glory days
at UCLA. Now we get to see more deeply into his Christian faith.
Thank you, Coach, for completing your legacy.

David Robinson
1987 WOODEN AWARD WINNER
10-TIME NBA ALL-STAR AND 1995 NBA MVP, SAN ANTONIO SPURS

Coach and Carty—this combination is a slam dunk. Coach John Wooden
is a great man of honor who is finishing well in the Lord; Jay Carty's
writing and speaking have touched the lives of hundreds of thousands.
They love Jesus, know hoops, have great insights and have earned the right
to be heard. *Coach Wooden: One-on-One* is a life-changing read.

Ricky Ryan
UNITED STATES SURFING CHAMPION, 1964
PASTOR, CALVARY CHAPEL
SANTA BARBARA, CALIFORNIA

Through the years the Fellowship of Christian Athletes has been honored
to be associated with Coach Wooden. Coach has been one of FCA's
cornerstone coaches, and we honor him each year during the NCAA Men's
Final Four Legends of the Hardwood Breakfast by presenting an award in
his name. Many times he has encouraged and challenged us, not only with
his stories of success, but also with his great model of faith. Now he has
put his life-shaping lessons and principles in this wonderful book. What a
great way for any athlete or coach to start his or her day!

Dal Shealy
PRESIDENT AND CEO
FELLOWSHIP OF CHRISTIAN ATHLETES

John Wooden dignified the game of basketball as a player, as a coach and even more as a gracious and uncommonly wise human being. I consider it a privilege to have known him as a competitor and a friend.

Coach Dean Smith
FORMER HEAD COACH, MEN'S BASKETBALL
UNIVERSITY OF NORTH CAROLINA

Coaching and living in Kentucky, I know how important God and basketball are to the people here. When things do not go right on the court, we have to learn how to make the best of the situation. When things don't go right in life, we must do the same. Coach Wooden, who became a legend at another school with a rich basketball tradition, has taught me so much about how to handle all situations on the court. But he has also shown me how to keep everything in perspective. After reading this book, I now have an even better grip on that bigger picture.

Tubby Smith
MEN'S BASKETBALL HEAD COACH
UNIVERSITY OF KENTUCKY

John Wooden taught us how to be the best we could be yet remain true to ourselves. Coach never asked us about our religion or our politics; he always felt that those were personal issues. But it was impossible not to know that he had an intensely strong and unshakable faith in God and that he drew upon the Bible for many of the principles by which he lived. As a result, his sacrifice, patience and devotion are the greatest examples and influences I have had in my life. If you allow the insights and reflections in this book to have even a measure of the impact on your life that Coach had on mine, you will be on your way to becoming the best person you can be.

Bill Walton
NBA ALL-STAR AND UCLA ALL-AMERICAN
NBC BASKETBALL ANNOUNCER

Compile a list of great Americans, using any criteria you wish. Base it on achievement, integrity, intelligence, wit, humility, number of people influenced in a positive way, devotion to family—whatever. John Wooden must be on the list!

Paul Westphal
NBA ALL-STAR, AND FORMER NBA COACH
HEAD COACH, MEN'S BASKETBALL
PEPPERDINE UNIVERSITY

John Wooden is the greatest basketball coach of all time. However, he is an even greater human being, and his wisdom about being successful in life is unmatched. Jay Carty has a unique ability to apply the principles of the Bible to our everyday life. The combination of John Wooden and Jay Carty in one book is too good to be true. Read this powerful material, apply it to your life, and spread the word to others.

Pat Williams
SENIOR VICE PRESIDENT
ORLANDO MAGIC

Coach Wooden is my friend and a great mentor. I've admired him as a coach but even more as a person. Other books have told of his coaching accomplishments, but *Coach Wooden: One-on-One* lets us look at the person and his faith. Thanks, Coach, for being a great example.

Roy Williams
HEAD MEN'S BASKETBALL COACH
UNIVERSITY OF NORTH CAROLINA

COACH
WOODEN
ONE-ON-ONE

JOHN WOODEN
JAY CARTY

Regal

From Gospel Light
Ventura, California, U.S.A.

PUBLISHED BY REGAL BOOKS
FROM GOSPEL LIGHT
VENTURA, CALIFORNIA, U.S.A.
Regal PRINTED IN THE U.S.A.

Regal Books is a ministry of Gospel Light, a Christian publisher dedicated to serving the local church. We believe God's vision for Gospel Light is to provide church leaders with biblical, user-friendly materials that will help them evangelize, disciple and minister to children, youth and families.

It is our prayer that this Regal book will help you discover biblical truth for your own life and help you meet the needs of others. May God richly bless you.

For a free catalog of resources from Regal Books/Gospel Light, please call your Christian supplier or contact us at 1-800-4-GOSPEL *or* www.regalbooks.com.

All Scripture quotations, unless otherwise indicated, are taken from the *Holy Bible*, New Living Translation, copyright © 1996. Used by permission of Tyndale House Publishers, Inc., Wheaton, Illinois 60189. All rights reserved.

Other versions used are
CEV—Contemporary English Version. Copyright © American Bible Society, 1995.
KJV—King James Version. Authorized King James Version.
THE MESSAGE—Scripture taken from *THE MESSAGE*. Copyright © by Eugene H. Peterson, 1993, 1994, 1995. Used by permission of NavPress Publishing Group.
NASB—Scripture taken from the *New American Standard Bible*, © 1960, 1962, 1963, 1968, 1971, 1972, 1973, 1975, 1977 by The Lockman Foundation. Used by permission.
NIV—Scripture taken from the *Holy Bible, New International Version*®. Copyright © 1973, 1978, 1984 by International Bible Society. Used by permission of Zondervan Publishing House. All rights reserved.

Cover and interior design by Robert Williams
Edited by Steven Lawson
Front cover photo © ASUCLA
Back cover photo by Kyle Duncan

Library of Congress Cataloging-in-Publication Data

Wooden, John R.
    Coach Wooden : one-on-one / John Wooden and Jay Carty.
        p. cm.
    ISBN 0-8307-3291-8
    1. Devotional calendars. I. Carty, Jay. II. Title.
    BV4811.W673 2003
    242'.2—dc21   2003013408

3 4 5 6 7 8 9 10 11 12 13 14 15 16 17 / 12 11 10 09 08 07 06 05 04

Any omission of credits is unintentional. The publisher requests documentation for future printings.

Rights for publishing this book in other languages are contracted by Gospel Light Worldwide, the international nonprofit ministry of Gospel Light. Gospel Light Worldwide also provides publishing and technical assistance to international publishers dedicated to producing Sunday School and Vacation Bible School curricula and books in the languages of the world. For additional information, visit www.gospellightworldwide.org; write to Gospel Light Worldwide, P.O. Box 3875, Ventura, CA 93006; or send an e-mail to info@gospellightworldwide.org.

DEDICATION

From John Wooden
to
Joshua Wooden, my father

Without you I would not be the person I am today. Thank you for
instilling in me the principles by which I have tried to live.

From Jay Carty
to
Mele

Full of joy and love, devoted to your children and wholly committed to God,
you consistently and continually wear the countenance of Christ. Thank you
for rubbing off on me for almost fifty years. It's been fun. I love you.

*There are many virtuous and capable women in the world,
but you surpass them all!*

PROVERBS 31:29

CONTENTS

ACKNOWLEDGMENTS

Special thanks from
Jay Carty
to Sam Talbert
(my Paul)

My dear friend, thank you for making sure the verses we chose
were appropriate to the lessons we wanted to teach.

A friend loves at all times.
Proverbs 17:17, *NASB*

Thanks from Jay and Coach to
Kyle Duncan (our publisher), Steven Lawson (our editor),
Robert Williams (our designer)
and the entire Regal team

Thank you, Kyle, for carrying this vision to fruition. You believed
in us and made this project happen. Thank you, Steve, for making
the process painless. You kept us from saying some things we
shouldn't say and you helped us say some things we should. We're
grateful. Rob, the cover is great! Thank you to the entire
Regal team—you are consummate professionals.

As iron sharpens iron, a friend sharpens a friend.
Proverbs 27:17

Special thanks from Jay to Wen Roberts for providing the photos
of me when I was on the Lakers and for all the memories that
came with them. Thanks also to Jim Fenk, Oregon State
University basketball publicist, for permission to use the OSU
photo and to Scott Quintard, Associated Services, University of
California at Los Angeles (ASUCLA) photography department, for
providing the historical photos of the Wooden era.

INTRODUCTION
BREAKFAST WITH COACH

If you stop by VIPs on Ventura Boulevard in Tarzana around eight o'clock any morning, you'll find what Andy Hill describes as a *Cheers* kind of place, "except everyone is over sixty and they're eating ham and eggs instead of drinking beer."[1] Paul or Lucy put most of their guests out front—but not their regulars, like Coach.

When the regulars enter, they turn left. If you come in with Coach, he'll introduce you to everyone. As you walk, you'll pass a counter on your right where a few folks will be seated on stools that spin. On your left you will see five vinyl-clad four-person booths. If you keep going, you will end up at the rest rooms, way in the back.

At the counter, on those stools that spin, you'll find Jerry, Scotty, Mike, Gene, Barbara and Lois, in that order. For some reason Jackie no longer comes, so that leaves three empties.

Anyone can occupy the first two booths. Ed and Margaret will be in the third one. In the far booth, you'll find Millie. Coach will take you to the fourth. Dick, Coach's son-in-law, will usually already be there. Tony will sit with Dick on Mondays, Wednesdays and Fridays. The fourth spot is for whoever accompanies Coach. That person could be anyone: a former player, someone wanting an interview or maybe a local high school coach.

If you are with Coach, you will sit next to him. Today Gloria is our server. On another day, it might be Stephanie. They both know Coach will order last. Coach asks me to "say a word," so I offer the blessing. Then we eat and chat. The first time you're there, don't try to pay the tab. Coach won't let you. He did let me get it the second time. That is the way of doing things with him.

At this writing, Coach John Wooden is almost ninety-three years old and his parts are beginning to break down. He's got two bad knees and an artificial hip that gives him fits—it's a toss-up as to which one is worse. He painfully gets out of a chair, takes a while to straighten up, uses a cane and moves slowly—his body a bit bent but not his mind. It's as straight as ever and crystal clear.

Coach still drives but only when he has to. The point is, he can. His car is a 1989 Taurus sedan, and he's proud to let you know that he got it in 1988 and it's only got 31,000 miles on it. It's perfect. Bill Hicks, one of his former players, runs a car dealership fifty miles away in Ventura. Once every three months Bill sends his assistant, Red, over to pick up the car and drive it back to the shop for service. They put more miles on the car servicing it than Coach does driving it.

I had breakfast with Coach as a result of reading Andy Hill's book *Be Quick but Don't Hurry*. Andy played for Coach at UCLA. Later he penned this fabulous work about reconciliation and the application of Coach's basketball principles to the business arena. The idea for his book was birthed while having breakfast with Coach.

I had just finished reading Andy's book when Eddie Sheldrake, a friend and another former Bruin player, called. In the course of the conversation I mentioned that I hadn't seen Coach for a while.

It had actually been a couple of years since I had seen Coach, the last time being at a UCLA players' function. Although I hadn't played for the Bruins (I played at Oregon State), I had been on Coach's staff at UCLA for three years. As far as I know, I am one of the few guys whom he considers one of his boys but didn't play on one of his teams. As a former coach, I am invited to the players' functions. Prior to that, we saw each other at a couple of weddings, and twice I prayed with him shortly after Nell, his beloved wife of fifty-three years, died.

So taking a lead from Andy and a prompting from Eddie, I called Coach and asked him if I could join him for breakfast. I didn't have an agenda at the time, but I got the idea for this book shortly thereafter.

Having already written six books, I still wanted to compile a collection of inspirational readings. I wanted to call it *Morning Meeties*, package it like a cereal box and use it to get kids to read about God while they ate their cereal. I talked to six publishers about it. I was the only one who thought it was a good idea.

However, after I had breakfast with Coach, it hit me: People know John Wooden is the greatest coach in the history of sports. Ten NCAA championships in twelve years set him apart from whoever is second. Perhaps people know him from his books *They Call Me Coach* or *Wooden*. If so, they'll know his background in Indiana at Purdue and Indiana State, his glory years at UCLA and his coaching and teaching philosophy. They might even know that he is one of the two people inducted into the Basketball Hall of Fame as both a player and a coach. But most people don't know much about John Wooden's spiritual side.

Coach has always preached the importance of balance, yet there is a spiritual dimension about the man that few know about. I'd like his legacy to be, for want of a better term, "more balanced," or at least more complete.

That is why I asked Coach to join me on this project.

As I began the interviewing process, the biggest concern Coach had was that he might appear to be something he is not. He doesn't want you to think he is a theologian. He's not, and I won't try to make you think he is. He says he is not a dynamic student of the Bible. By academic standards, he's right. But his dad read to him from the Word of God almost every day of his youth; he read it with his wife, Nellie, almost every day of their marriage; and he has read from it almost every day since she went to be with the Lord. He may not be an academic, but he is a practicer who knows the difference between trying to work your way to heaven and accepting forgiveness through Jesus Christ. His Bible is frayed, dog-eared and marked up. It didn't get that way by sitting on a shelf.

Coach usually prays before he goes to bed and when he gets up in the morning. He also shoots up short "arrow prayers" during the course of the day. I think he assumes that everyone does the same, so it is not a big deal and is not worthy of mention. He doesn't realize how unusual he is in that regard, because everyone doesn't do those things. And not many people have stated their philosophy of life in a way that is so winsome and attractive in this world riddled by political correctness. Coach John Wooden has been successful in every sense of the word. This success can be traced to his philosophy of life, which is solidly based on biblical principles.

Coach Wooden says that during his ninety-two-plus years he has had his spiritual ups and downs. "I'm ashamed to say I've fallen short," he admits, "but my desire has been to 'walk the talk.'" It's a cliché, but at ninety-two he's earned the right to use it.

In this book, Coach gives us glimpses into the spiritual part of his world. I think you will find these peeks to be refreshing. I follow his words with a few of my own. My goal as cowriter has been to reflect on his thoughts, principles and experiences. Sometimes I do this by sharing an experience of my own; other times I draw an illustration from the Bible.

This book is broken up into sixty individual readings. Each one is short—a perfect start to each day (but you can read them anytime). Each reading begins with a Bible verse. Then you go one-on-one with Coach. Next, you go one-on-one with me. Finally, you have an opportunity to pray and read a few more Scriptures—that is when you go one-on-one with God. Imagine the four of us sitting in a booth at VIPs: you, Coach, me and God. Get yourself a Bible, so you can read the recommended verses each day.

For the next sixty days, I invite you to join us as we go one-on-one.

Jay Carty

WOODEN CARTY

ONE-ON-ONE

86,400 Seconds

So be careful how you live, not as fools but as those who are wise.
Make the most of every opportunity for doing good in these evil days.

EPHESIANS 5:15-16

Time lost is time lost. It's gone forever. Some people tell themselves that they will work twice as hard tomorrow to make up for what they did not do today. People should always do their best. If they can work twice as hard tomorrow, then they should have also worked twice as hard today. That would have been their best. Catching up leaves no room for them to do their best tomorrow. People with the philosophy of putting off and then working twice as hard cheat themselves.

Most young people don't know how to work hard, and so many are satisfied with just getting by. I wouldn't settle for this second-best attitude from my players. I'd ask them, "If you do not have the time to do it right the first time, when will you find the time to do it over?"

I sought to help my players learn to work hard in three areas of life: Certainly, I wanted to help them get the most out of themselves physically, but I also wanted them to learn to work hard mentally and emotionally. I asked that their studies come first, basketball second and social lives third. This required them to have discipline. Physical conditioning, of course, was needed to play basketball, but it also helped them gain control in other areas.

To do a good job on their studies, they needed to develop mental control. As a result, most of my players graduated. To avoid mistakes and stay focused, they also needed to have emotional control. Achieving that takes hard work. Control in all three areas helped my players keep focus in school, on the court and in life.

–JW

If every morning your bank credited your account with $86,400 but every evening canceled whatever part of the amount you failed to use, what would you do? Spend every cent—of course!

Well, you have such a bank account—it is called time. Every day it credits you with 86,400 seconds. At midnight, whatever you failed to use is lost. A balance is not carried over to the next day and you're not allowed overdrafts. Each day the bank named Time opens a new account with you. Each night it burns the records of the day. If you fail to use the day's deposits, the loss is yours.

That is Christian comedian Robert G. Lee's take on time. I like it. It helps me put value into each day. The apostle Paul also had a take on time. He wrote to the Christians of a city called Ephesus and suggested that they make each day a masterpiece. A wise person, he pointed out, will make the most of his or her time.

To truly make each day a masterpiece, we must first understand the Lord's will. If we are going to grasp His plan, then we need to know it, so a good way to start each day is reading the Bible. For greater understanding, pray about what you read.

You can't have a masterpiece if you spend time on frivolous activities or outright sin. Paul wrote about the problem of addiction to alcohol, but he could have added drugs, porn, food and online chatrooms to his list of detrimental time wasters. How many hours do you spend each day on these or other unhealthy habits? How could you better use that time?

Finally, Paul urges us to be filled with the Spirit. Having God's power helps us say no to the bad stuff and yes to God's will. How will you spend your 86,400 seconds today? How can you make today a masterpiece?

–GC

Dear Lord God, I want today to be a masterpiece for You.
I want to bring glory to You every minute of the day.
May it be so.

Forever Young

Wisdom belongs to the aged, and understanding to those who have lived many years.

JOB 12:12

I try to read something every day. I always read some Scripture. Then I go to the newspaper. I first turn to the headlines on the front page to look for anything that's of interest. Then before going to the sports page—which many think I'd go to first—I look at the crossword puzzle. Later in the day I will work on that. Then I glance at the bridge hand. There was a time when I enjoyed playing bridge. I read these sections to keep up-to-date. Then I turn to the sports page. I skim it before breakfast and then read it thoroughly after I have eaten.

The newspaper is not the only thing I read. I enjoy new books. I'll read at least one a month. There was a time when I did a lot more—that is when I could read faster and could retain better than I can today. Of course, all of my reading is the printed word—the old-fashioned way, I guess. The Internet is a nice idea, but it came along too late for me to take much advantage of it.

While I am losing my abilities, and technology has zoomed past me, I'm not going to get upset. It's the natural, normal way of life. I accept the reality; nevertheless, I still want to operate to the best of my abilities. I will continue to do the best I can with what I have. I won't stand still. I will always try to move forward. I want to keep learning. I want to function as well as I am capable of functioning. Whatever comes out of that comes out of that. It will be a by-product of always striving to be the best I can be.

–JW

Baseball player Satchel Paige once asked, "How old would you be if you didn't know how old you was?"[1] Oliver Wendell Holmes put it this way: "To be seventy years young is sometimes far more cheerful and hopeful than to be forty years old."[2]

I wholeheartedly agree and my grandkids will attest to that. I would hate it if there were anything my grandkids wanted to do that I was too stuffy or *old* to try. If my body won't let me do a particular feat, that's one problem; but if my attitude won't let me proceed, that's quite another.

One of my great joys in life was chasing through the tubes and sliding down the chutes in a fun house with Anna, my granddaughter. I wasn't the only adult frolicking about, but I was the oldest and definitely the biggest. I didn't even mind sliding into the plastic balls and getting completely covered up. My grandkids think I'm fun. Ride roller coasters at Six Flags? Sure! Paint each other's faces, do projects with glitter, or color with the mega big box of Crayolas? You bet! Color outside the lines? Always! I'm definitely an out-of-the-box-type person. Not in a rebellious way. Not in a sinful way. But life to the fullest is best lived outside the lines. Older people often have way too many lines. And I'm not talking about the ones they wear on the outside.

In May 2002, at sixty years of age, I contracted a permanently paralyzed vocal cord. A virus killed it. After 25 years of preaching, it was all over in a moment. My work had also been my passion and my hobby. I could no longer do it. It would have been very easy to take the disability checks and retire. But that is not what Coach taught me. I decided to keep developing. This book is the result. I plan to continue to be the best I can be, no matter my circumstances or my age.

–JC

Heavenly Father, give me the courage to expand
my boundaries, to learn to glorify God outside the lines
and to pursue becoming all I am capable of becoming,
regardless of my age or circumstances. Amen.

TODAY'S READING: PSALMS 90:10; 92:14; PROVERBS 16:31; ISAIAH 46:4;
EXODUS 20:12; PSALM 34:12-13; PROVERBS 3:1-2; 1 PETER 3:10-11

The Greatest Word

Pay all your debts, except the debt of love for others.
You can never finish paying that! If you love your neighbor,
you will fulfill all the requirements of God's law.

Love" is the greatest word in our language. When we have love, many of our problems disappear. Differences are manageable when love has its way. I'm sure my regard for love comes from my reading of the Bible, specifically the love chapter, 1 Corinthians 13, which is my favorite passage. We can give without loving, but we can't love without giving. In fact, love is nothing unless we give it to someone.

I like to visit the veterans' hospital and I go to children's hospitals as well. I've always had a particular love and empathy for children. I have cherished times when I have been able to hold a newborn in my arms. I especially remember holding astronaut Sally Ride and Stanford basketball coach Mike Montgomery when they were babies.

I was pleased when the organizers of the Wooden Classic Basketball Tournament decided to give a portion of their proceeds to children's hospitals. Now they have money going to the Special Olympics, and that pleases me, too. Needs of children have a special appeal to me. Showing love for these children through these gifts makes me very happy. I know the money doesn't make all of their problems disappear, but it certainly helps make their lives better.

–JW

My grandchildren amaze me. When Matthew was six he hooked up a DVD player without any help and was watching a children's program when his dad got home. Yikes! I still can't program my old VCR.

Anna has always had a way with words. When she was just four, she was talking about God with her mom. The conversation went something like this:

Anna: Nobody knows what God looks like except Grandpa Robbie. He sees His face. Do you think He'll have a round face like this? (*Circles her own face with her finger.*) With longer legs? Do you think God can hang upside down and touch the earth? He is the true God, so He can do anything! Is what I'm saying too precious so that you might have to cry? He's the true King; He'll never let us down. He won't fail us. He loves us. He won't even fail the parents. He loves the grandmas, grandpas, mommies, daddies, children, brothers and sisters. Even the people who are eighty. And the people who are gonna die. Right? He loves everybody. He even likes everybody. He's the one true goodest King. Do you know why?

Mom (*Scrambling for a quick answer about the intrinsic nature of the goodness of God.*): Because He is the creator and He is good. Anything that is good is good because it is like God.

Anna: That's right big mama! Give me five!

God is love. Anna understands the concept. Coach understands it, too. But it's not easy to grasp. The Bible is clear: On our own, we can neither love God nor love people the way God does. But we can experience His love, and we can get so close to God that He will love others through us.

Coach has a close walk with God, and God loves people through him. Anna has the faith of a child, and God does the same with her. I can't hook up a VCR, and God still loves me and allows me to love others!

Is your walk with the Father so close that He regularly loves people through you?

–GC

*Father, I want to allow You to love my neighbor through me
with the same love that You love me. Amen.*

TODAY'S READING: ROMANS 13:8-10; 1 CORINTHIANS 13:1-13; 1 JOHN 4:7–5:3

God's Plan

"For I know the plans I have for you," says the LORD. *"They are plans for good and not for disaster, to give you a future and a hope."*

JEREMIAH 29:11

I haven't had any "God said" events that I can recall, but I have become aware of God's hand on my life. I can now look back to see that God was at work, especially in certain circumstances that at the time I thought were simply strokes of good luck.

In 1944, during World War II, I had orders to board the USS *Franklin* in the South Pacific. My orders were canceled due to an emergency surgery. My appendix ruptured. During an attack, the person who took my place was at the battle station where I would have been, and he was killed by a kamikaze.

Years later I had to travel from Atlanta to Raleigh for a summer basketball camp at Campbell College. I usually went on a Saturday, but I couldn't leave at that time because of a conflict. I had my ticket, but I had to cancel and book the same flight for the following day. The Saturday flight—the one I was supposed to be on—crashed and everyone on board was killed. Flying over the crash site the next day made me consider the spiritual nature of life. I thought deeply about God and His plans and wondered why He had spared me.

One such incident might be considered luck, if a person believed in luck. But twice to be so overtly delivered from death caused me to pause and ponder. I could not dismiss it as a mere coincidence. No, it was more likely God's hand at work in my life than luck. He had plans for me.

–JW

With tears in his eyes Coach asked me, "Why does God allow awful things to happen, especially to children? Why the children?" The answer lies in the importance of our free will.

I have to admit that theologically it is easier for me to explain why God rarely intervenes than why He sometimes does. God gave us free will—we get to make choices that matter—and He rarely violates the consequences of our choices.

I know this does not fully answer the question, but the important point here is that God doesn't want to intervene, yet there are times when He does. Why? Perhaps it is because He has plans for us. Yet each of us has a free will. How can we have a free will to choose our own way when God has plans for our lives? I don't pretend to have a clue as to how it all works. It's very confusing, but that's the way God does it. Isn't that just like Him? He loves acting in ways that will increase our faith—like making good out of bad.

God doesn't promise to make all bad events good. But He does promise to make something good come out of a bad situation if we will love and trust Him. After preaching for twenty-five years, I contracted a paralyzed vocal cord. I haven't addressed an audience since May 2002.

I believe one of the reasons God spared John Wooden those many years ago and why I have a broken voice is so we could combine to put together a message for you through this book. It is part of God's plan. And that line of thinking begs the question, What has God done in your life to put this book in your hands?

We hope you are drawn closer to the master, because God has plans for you, too.

–*JC*

Creator God, I don't understand how all this works,
but thank You for the plans You have for me.
Help me to walk the path You have laid out and let me
bring glory to Your name. Amen.

TODAY'S READING: JEREMIAH 29:11-13; JAMES 4:13-15; EPHESIANS 1:9-12

Such a Time as This

And we know that God causes everything to work together for the good of those who love God and are called according to his purpose for them.

ROMANS 8:28

I've been the closest to the Lord at the birth of my two children and when, after ninety-one days in a complete coma, my wife, Nellie, squeezed my hand, opened her eyes and had a wonderful expression on her face that I can still see in my mind's eye. It was a tremendous feeling. I tingled all over. It was far more than mere emotion. The whole experience was deeply spiritual.

In 1982, Nellie had replacement hip surgery. In the middle of the operation, she had a heart attack and went into a coma. After three months, she came to and I was able to take her home.

Gradually she got better, although she never completely recovered. On Christmas Eve 1984, we went to my daughter Nan's, and the whole family was there. Nellie was happy. We had a nice evening. A measure of quality had returned to her life. After I brought her home, around one in the morning, she got real bad. I took her back to the hospital and she never came out. Nellie was in and out of a coma until March 21, 1985. I lost her on Nan's birthday. God relieved Nellie of her suffering and I lost my life partner.

I love to read Charles Dickens, so I will paraphrase here the opening of his *Tale of Two Cities*: Nellie and I had seen the best times; for me, losing her was one of the worst of times.

-JW

I have been a traveling preacher for almost twenty-five years. Then, as I already noted, in early 2002, I contracted a paralyzed vocal cord. I haven't addressed an audience since. I can speak conversationally for short periods and that's it. I assumed my contribution to the Kingdom had been significantly minimized.

I've always preached that my job is what I call vertical relationship and God's job is horizontal influence. So if He wanted to restrict my ability to relate with people, that was His business, and I wouldn't fight Him. Instead, I would be ready to walk through whatever new doors God would open before me. Writing is one of them. Being a better, more attentive grandfather is another. Who knows what else God might have planned.

It's the same with Coach. With the loss of his dear wife, his reflections back on his life and his increasing willingness to share his faith, he will probably impact more people for Christ at ninety-two than at any other point in his life. Again, God moved Coach past a very hard time to a greater good.

In both of our cases, God used tragedy and loss to prepare us for such a time as this. When we are weak, He is strong. I can't talk and Coach is old, so we qualify. We love God and the result is that He has made even our tragedies work together for good. Indeed, when we could have been mired in the worst of times, God has taken us to the best of times.

–JC

Almighty God, I trust You to make something good come out of whatever tragedies befall me. Thank You for caring about me. I entrust my day to You. Amen.

TODAY'S READING: 1 CORINTHIANS 1:26-29; 2 CORINTHIANS 4:16–5:10; 12:9; ROMANS 8:28

Rock-solid roots: Coach's father, Joshua (above left), and his mother, Roxie Anna (above right), pointed their sons toward paths of success. At Purdue Coach excelled on the basketball court as an All-American (left) and in the classroom as an academic achiever (bottom left).

© ASUCLA

Family first: John and Nell Wooden (opposite page, bottom right) established a legacy at home. In 1998, years after Nell's death, the entire clan gathered to honor Coach (above). Nancy and Jim (below left) carry the Wooden torch to the next generation, which includes Wooden's seven grandchildren—three of whom relax with Nancy (below right).

First Things First

That night God appeared to Solomon in a dream and said,
"What do you want? Ask, and I will give it to you!"

2 CHRONICLES 1:7

Don't let making a living prevent you from making a life. People don't spend enough time with their families. They get caught up in material things, thinking those make up life. The pursuit of material possessions often takes precedence over the things that are more lasting, such as faith, family and friends. Don't allow the lesser values to raise havoc on your family.

Earlier in life, I put family in front of faith. I've fixed that. But I always tried to keep work fourth on the list. I was proud when Nellie told an interviewer, "I never could tell whether John had a good practice or a bad practice, because he never brought it home."

I put faith first now, but this poem written by one of my former players, Swen Nater, reads better with the order changed. I think God will understand.

Family, Faith and Friends
Give me family, faith, and friends; they're all I'll ever love
They're all I'll crave from crib to grave and all I'll bring above.
Give me family, faith, and friends, above prosperity
For wealth untold and fleeting gold do not appeal to me.

Give me family, faith and friends, not notoriety
To have a name with worldly fame does not compare you see.
Give me family, faith and friends; they're my priority
I'll be well known among my own and rich I'll surely be.

Swen attached this note to the poem: "Dearest Coach and Teacher, you lived this. For that I will ever be grateful."

–JW

Solomon didn't find a bottle on the beach and rub it. He didn't get a "big poof"! There was no genie. Neither was he limited to three wishes. God visited him one night and asked, "What do you want? Ask, and I will give it to you!" God gave His Visa card to Solomon and told him to have at it.

What would you do if you won the lottery? Perhaps you think that your winnings would make you truly happy. Maybe you believe the freedom from work would give you time for your spouse or kids. Did you know that over 70 percent of big lottery winners end up getting a divorce within two years? Now that you know, I'll bet you'd still like to win and take your chances at being one of the 30 percent. If you are single, you probably would risk being able to find someone who would want you and not just your money. Do you really want to play those kind of odds?

Why do you want to win the lottery? If you won, how would it affect your faith, your family and your friends? If you hit the jackpot, how would you then make your life?

I can make you a promise. If you're not happy with your faith, family and friends now, money won't make you happy later. But given the opportunity, there are few who would pass on the cash and choose what Solomon chose: "Give me wisdom and knowledge to rule them properly, for who is able to govern this great nation of yours?"[1] Solomon put his position, his responsibility and the people ahead of his own welfare. And because God could trust him with wealth, He gave that to him, too.

The greatest blessings come from keeping the right priorities. Today, let's put first things first.

–*GC*

O God, I ask two favors from you before I die.
First, help me never to tell a lie.
Second, give me neither poverty nor riches!
Give me just enough to satisfy my needs.
For if I grow rich, I may deny you and say,
"Who is the LORD?" And if I am too poor, I may steal
and thus insult God's holy name.

TODAY'S READING: PROVERBS 30:7-9 (WHICH IS THE TEXT OF TODAY'S PRAYER); 2 CHRONICLES 1:7-13; PROVERBS 3:5-6; MATTHEW 6:19-34

Questioning God

In spite of everything, Job did not sin or accuse God of doing wrong.

JOB 1:22, CEV

My faith has never failed, but grief has been cause for me to question God three times in my life. The first time was when Nellie died. We had been married for fifty-three years. She was the only girl I ever dated. It took me a little more than two years to get past her death. I've never gotten over it.

The second was when my great-grandson was born with birth disorders. My granddaughter is very strong and I'm grateful for her, but the circumstance caused me to question.

The third was when my younger brother died. He was sick, but I didn't think it was that serious. I was holding his hand when he took his last breath. It caught me by surprise. Again, I questioned God. I never doubted God's existence or my relationship with Him, but in my grief, I questioned His actions.

I've always taught the importance of keeping our emotions under control, but we must deal with grief when it comes. Grief controlled me for a season, and that's natural, I suppose. When grief passed, so did the questions. I was able to get back to the reality that God is far greater than I am and to see that I must accept His actions, even if I do not understand them at the time.

–JW

During biblical times, the reaction to the loss of a loved one took a variety of forms. Mourning could include dressing in black, covering the head, wearing sackcloth, putting ashes or olive oil on one's head, tearing one's garments or hiring professional mourners to help with the wailing, weeping, crying and screaming. Not only was grief permissible, but it was also expected. Even Jesus wept: He cried over the death of Lazarus. Many of the expressions of the times were cultural rather than biblical. Through the centuries, whatever the outward expression, the inward act of grieving over significant loss is a human necessity. However, I'm glad we don't do oil, ashes and sackcloth anymore.

Job is an Old Testament character who lost everything but his wife—he also got boils as a bonus. Despite all of this, Job did not blame God. He was handling his tough circumstances just fine until what was left of his family and friends grew tired of waiting for improvement. "Curse God and die" was his wife's advice. Compassion wasn't her gift.

After seven days of sitting silently with Job, his friends started grumbling, too. It was more than he could handle. Job finally caved in and asked God, "Why me? What'd I do?"

God said, "Why not you?" Then He promptly took Job to the woodshed for a good talkin' to and gave him a time-out. Job pleased God by repenting. Job had questioned God while he grieved, but he hadn't tried to be God. Coach did the same thing when he grieved and questioned.

There is a big difference between screaming "God, just what do You think you're doin'!" and asking "God, what's going on?" God won't tolerate the former. He understands and responds to the latter.

—JC

Father, forgive me when my lack of understanding
raises questions I have no business asking.
Deepen my faith and move me forward in my
walk with You. Thank You, Lord.

TODAY'S READING: JOB 1:13–2:10; 38:1-7; 40:3-9; 42:10

The Strength of Gentleness

The Lord's servants must not quarrel but must be kind to everyone. They must be able to teach effectively and be patient with difficult people.

2 TIMOTHY 2:24

Abraham Lincoln once wrote about the importance of having "a gentle, but firm, and certain hand."[1] The Chinese writer and physician Han Suyin put it this way: "There is nothing stronger in the world than gentleness."[2] Those words make me think of my father.

My dad influenced me in many ways. He was physically strong, but he wasn't a huge man. Because he knew how to use his leverage, he could lift and move things around that stronger people could not. He was powerful, but he was also kind and gentle.

I never heard him say an unkind word about anyone, nor did I ever hear him utter a word of profanity. I saw my dad's gentle spirit on display when he worked with fractious horses and with dogs I thought were vicious.

I remember a young man whipping a short-tempered team of horses, trying to get them to come out of a gravel pit. They were pulling against each other, jumping back and forth, fretting and stomping. My dad went to the boy and said, "Let me take 'em."

He stood amongst them. He got his head between their heads as they continued sweating, fretting and stomping. By talking to each of them and patting them, he quieted them down. Then he went behind them and took the reins, let go, and they immediately pulled out together. His gentleness made all the difference.

There is nothing stronger than gentleness. My dad was the epitome of this principle.

—JW

Imagine with me a new reality show. You're the contestant and they send you into a dark alley, filming all along. You're halfway through the passage when four big, ugly guys emerge. They enter the alley through a shadowy door, turn in your direction and start to approach. You find yourself cornered. Make the guys Hell's Angels, skinheads, drug dealers, gangbangers, Kung-Fu-type martial arts experts or drug lords—whatever would put the most fear into you.

Viewers would be on the edge of their seats, hoping to see you get thumped—after all, our society loves violence. Suddenly, you notice that each man carries a Bible; and you hear someone yell from the open door, "Thanks for coming to the Bible study, fellas. See you next week. God bless."

How did the presence of the Bibles and the realization these men are coming from a Bible study affect you? Did you stop worrying? Why wouldn't people watch a show like that? Gentleness doesn't sell. We admire power, assertiveness and World Wrestling Entertainment.

People today do not teach their children to aspire to be the gentlest kids in the neighborhood. We generally teach them that nice guys finish last. We are a me-first generation. But is this right? Coach Wooden never put himself first, yet he didn't finish last. He's a winner, and he won with class. He didn't get angry, he didn't use profanity, and he didn't provoke people. John Wooden is gentle and he is a gentleman.

The gentleness of Jesus shaped Joshua Wooden's world. Joshua Wooden, in turn, shaped his son. Coach then shaped his players with that same gentle approach and molded a generation of young people. If we learn the gentleness of Jesus, we too can shape our world.

–*JC*

Dear Lord, teach me to control my tongue,
my mind and my emotions.
Teach me how to have the
gentleness of Jesus. Thank You.

TODAY'S READING: EPHESIANS 4:25—5:2; 2 TIMOTHY 2:24; 1 THESSALONIANS 2:7

The Blessing

My child, never forget the things I have taught you.
Store my commands in your heart.

PROVERBS 3:1

When I graduated from a small country grade school, my father gave me two things. One was a two-dollar bill. He said, "As long as you keep this, you'll never be broke." He also gave me a card. On one side was a verse by Henry Van Dyke:

Four things a man must learn to do
If he would make his life more true:
To think without confusion clearly,
To love his fellow-man sincerely,
To act from honest motives purely,
To trust in God and Heaven securely.

On the other side, was Dad's seven-point creed:

1. Be true to yourself.
2. Help others.
3. Make each day your masterpiece.
4. Drink deeply from good books, especially the Bible.
5. Make friendship a fine art.
6. Build a shelter against a rainy day.
7. Pray for guidance and count and give thanks for your blessings every day.

All my dad said when he gave me the note was, "Son, try and live up to these things." It didn't mean as much to me in those early days as it came to mean later in life. I carried that paper in my wallet until it wore out. I've had to copy it several times over the years, and I have a copy in my wallet today.

People ask me, "Have you lived up to that creed?"

I tell them, "No, I haven't always lived up to it. But I've tried!"

—JW

When your kids get into junior high, put them in a barrel and feed them through the knothole. When they get into high school, plug up the knothole. This is my variation of advice widely attributed to Mark Twain. I have repeated it often. The teenage years are so volatile that parents should not worry about making much progress. Everyone—the teen and the parents—does well just to make it through.

Joshua Wooden had earned the right to say some very important words to his teenaged son. Apparently Joshua's timing was also God's timing. His message was compelling and still has a shaping force nearly a century later.

It is important that parents bless their children. There is nothing greater that they can do for their sons and daughters. Joshua gave a blessing to John—powerful words, administered with a hug and lots of love.

"Don't consider yourself superior to anyone else, but never feel inferior," Joshua told his son. Then he gave him a battle plan and commissioned him to face the future with strength. The dad blessed his son with a blessing so meaningful it continues to shape and mold Coach John Wooden today.

God wants to bless you in the same way Joshua Wooden blessed his son. He wants you to receive His blessing and He wants you to be a blessing to others. As you go through this book, we believe a blessing is waiting for you in each reading. Will you receive the blessing and will you pass it on?

–GC

Father God, I accept Your blessing this day
and I will look for Your blessings each day
in the days ahead. Please show me
how to bless others. Amen.

Beautiful Within

Study this Book of the Law continually. Meditate on it day and night so you may be sure to obey all that is written in it. Only then will you succeed.

JOSHUA 1:8

I grew up on a farm. When I was in grade school, my dad, Joshua Wooden, would read to me and my brothers almost every evening. I can close my eyes and picture him. Because of Dad's emphasis on reading, all four of us boys majored or minored in English.

There's a lot of trash published, but there is a lot of good literature, too. Never buy a book because of its cover. It's what's inside that counts. I have a saying on my dining-room table: "Dear Lord, make me beautiful within." That's what I want from the books I read.

I have several bookcases. Three of them have words carved on the front. One reads "Drink Deeply from Good Books, Especially the Bible." My father read to us from the Bible every day when I was growing up. I continued that practice into college and throughout my life. My dear wife, Nellie, and I read God's Word together and we read it to our children. The other two bookcases are inscribed with the words "Balance" and "Love." If we all had love to the degree that we should, we would have no other problems. Regarding balance—it's the most important component in basketball, and it is a very important part of life. We must always keep things in perspective so that we can maintain emotional control.

I like historical novels and biographies. I enjoy poetry most of all. I prefer Victorian-era poets and I like the early American poets.

–JW

On a rural farm in Indiana eighty-five years ago, there wasn't a whole lot going on at night. A dad reading by the light of a kerosene lantern and a mom serving cookies hot out of the oven were the most exciting things going. The result was four Wooden boys who loved literature.

At the same age, I was eating dinner in front of the radio and listening to the classics of the late forties: *The Lone Ranger*, *The Cisco Kid* and *Inner Sanctum*. It wasn't long before television gave me Milton Berle and Howdy Doody. When I was in high school, I discovered classic comic books. I could scan them quickly and use them for my book reports. I didn't want anything to interrupt *American Bandstand*. The result: I didn't read much.

Today children read even less. The Internet and video games vie for time with television and hundreds of cable channels. As a result, young people have developed their fine motor skills and they know how to program a wall of home-entertainment electronics, but when it comes to reading, they have not been there nor have they done much of that.

I'm proud of my daughter, Kim. She is raising my two grandchildren without cable television. In the evenings, they do things together as a family. Their library cards are well used. They all read a lot. The children are developing an imagination. Their vocabulary and their ability to express themselves clearly demonstrate what I missed. Moreover, both of them enjoy letting God speak to them through His Word.

Reading is a lost art. I recommend that you fill yourself and your family with good books, especially the Bible. Check out books on tape from the library—play them when you take trips. You might even want to get rid of the television. Reading good books will make you beautiful within. And who knows? Someone might even whip up a batch of hot cookies.

–*GC*

Heavenly Father, I want to delight in filling
my mind with everything that would please You.
Night and day, I want to think
about Your Word. Amen.

Powerful Principles

I have fought a good fight, I have finished the race, and I have remained faithful.

2 TIMOTHY 4:7

My dad passed on powerful principles to me. He often used words that I have carried to this day. I will never forget a wonderful formula for success—two sets of three—he gave me when I was in grade school:

Don't lie.   Don't whine.
Don't cheat.   Don't complain.
Don't steal.   Don't make excuses.

He said, "If you never lie, you'll never have to remember what you said." Then he added, "Never try to be better than somebody else. Always learn from others and never cease trying to be the best you can be."

Doing our best really does define success. My father read this poem to me as a child and it has helped shape me through the years:

At God's footstool to confess,
A poor soul knelt and bowed his head.
"I failed," he cried. The master said,
"Thou didst thy best. That is success."[1]

I'm in my ninth decade. I wish I could tell you I lived up to my father's expectations. Rather, I'm more like John Newton who also acknowledged:

I am not what I ought to be,
I am not what I want to be,
I am not what I am going to be,
But I am thankful that
I am better than I used to be.[2]

I've never stopped trying to do what's right. I'm not doing it to earn favor with God. I'm doing it because it's the right thing to do. My earthly father and my heavenly Father would expect nothing less.

–JW

Stay faithful and finish well.

I often close my letters with that phrase. It's a summary of what I hope can be said about the rest of my life. Coach has used the two sets of three to stay on course and keep the faith. They sound reasonable, but are they biblical?

Jesus' reduction of the Ten Commandments encompasses Joshua Wooden's first set of three and then some. Lying, cheating and stealing are clearly sins, but what about the other three?

Joseph was sold into slavery by his brothers and thrown into jail unjustly. He didn't whine or complain. God rewarded him. Jacob tricked his brother, Esau, but a trickier trickster named Laban tricked the trickster. Jacob didn't whine or complain. God rewarded him. It was the same way with Job. He did just fine with all his troubles until he started whining and complaining. God got on his case. It appears that God doesn't like grousing, but what about making excuses?

What was the first thing Eve did after sinning? She blamed the snake. What's the first thing Adam did? He blamed Eve. When that didn't work, he blamed God. "It was the woman *You* gave me." So God gave them both the boot. He doesn't like excuses for sin.

We shouldn't lie, cheat or steal. Neither should we whine, complain or make excuses. Joshua Wooden was right on. His advice worked well for Coach. It will work well for you.

Stay faithful and finish well.

–JC

Dear Lord, guard me from sin—
especially from whining, complaining
and making excuses.
Help me to take what life brings
and trust in You. Amen.

Gutsy Gals

Her children stand and bless her. Her husband praises her: "There are many virtuous and capable women in the world, but you surpass them all!"

PROVERBS 31:28-29

The most important profession in the world is parenting. Parents are the first coaches a child has. Mine were wonderful. You know about my dad. Let me tell you a bit about my mom.

My mother, Roxie Anna, worked hard, long hours canning, cooking, sewing, mending, washing—it never ended. She had four sons and few conveniences, not even electricity or inside plumbing. I've often felt badly that I haven't spoken of her more often over the years. She made sure we were up for Sunday School and was a wonderful mother. In the evenings when we were resting on the porch, she would be making us treats.

Mother was an accomplished seamstress and did a lot of that kind of thing for others around town. She made most of her clothes—very few store-bought items hung in her closet. She made me my first basketball out of rags stuffed into old black cotton hose. As I think back, I swear I remember dribbling that thing. That is impossible, but I like to think I could have.

Mother was a woman of infinite patience, who worked very hard and never complained. She taught me that hard work is a part of life.

Life's most difficult burden for my mom was the loss of her two daughters, my sisters. Cordelia was three when she died of diphtheria. Another daughter died in infancy before she was named. Mom wanted a daughter desperately, and those two events hurt her more than anything else life threw at her. She carried a sense of loss on her shoulders forever.

All four of us boys were excellent students and if one of us got recognition for something, Mother was always careful to let people know something wonderful about the other three. She made sure that there was equality among us.

Proverbs 31 is about an excellent wife. All of the attributes mentioned in that passage apply to my mom.

–JW

I guess it's the pain of childbirth that bonds a woman to her baby in ways that a man can't understand. Mothers look at their newborn differently. They hold them more tenderly. Dads go through the roof when a teething infant bites on his finger. How do moms keep smiling and think it's cute when the baby is chewing on her nipple? Fathers love their children—but not like moms. A mother's love is in a league by itself.

"Mom" is mostly a two-syllable word. It is pronounced "maa-ahm" and it's usually used when a child wants something or when Mom won't let them do something. The word "mom" means love in action while dying for your kids as Christ died for you. That's Carty's Old-Geezer Translation, not Webster's. A synonym for mom is "gutsy gal."

There is rarely enough time, money or energy, yet moms go on. They seldom take moments for themselves. Kids and the husband demand total attention. Where do they find time to work and do the wash? How do they cope with the stress of going to the market and cleaning the house? And there are the endless practices and games and lessons. Their day ends mercifully when they pray with the kids, tuck them in and then go back to pick up a bit before pouring into bed. Then they do it all over again the next day and the day after that, with no letup in sight. That's right: no letup. And they have to do it on weekends, too. They never get a day off, and they won't for years. And they wonder where they'll get the strength to go on, yet they do somehow—with a smile.

I don't know how mothers do it. I'm amazed at their tenacity. They are incredible. Moms are truly gutsy gals.

—JC

May God give my gutsy gal the strength to endure,
the patience to persevere and the grace to enjoy
a measure of the fruit of the Spirit
as she serves our family. Amen.

TODAY'S READING: PROVERBS 31:10-31

Overcoming Adversity

Consider it a sheer gift, friends, when tests and challenges come at you from all sides.

JAMES 1:2, *THE MESSAGE*

When I was a boy, we were poor, but we had what we needed. We didn't think of our lack of material possessions as adversity. Looking back, I realize that times were tough, but I didn't think of it that way back then.

The pigs got cholera, the drought killed the crops, and we lost the farm, so we moved into town. We still didn't think of it as harsh conditions. It was just necessary. I guess many people who lived through the Great Depression and its aftermath view life that way.

As I entered adulthood, I faced the same kind of challenges my folks had faced and had to quickly learn to get along with very little. A few days before Nellie and I were to be married, a bank failure took my life savings of $909.05, which was a lot of money in those days. A friend loaned us some cash so that we could get married anyway. I left to fight in World War II, and when I returned, another financial problem awaited me: the bank had foreclosed on our home. My parents had shown me how to handle the setback, so we packed up and moved on. When I was on staff at Indiana State University, I was director of athletics, head basketball and baseball coach and taught courses. I also worked to finish my master's thesis. I look back and think, *How could I possibly have done all of that*! But I had not thought of it as a hardship at the time, and I never made excuses.

The more concerned we become over the things we can't control, the less we will do with the things we can control. My father often quoted Abraham Lincoln on this point: "We'd all be much happier if we magnified our blessings rather than our disappointments." I guess that's what we did.

–JW

Joshua Wooden faced hard times. So has John Wooden. How did they make it through? To understand better, let me tell you about sand and rocks.

How is sand made? Rocks hanging out at the beach day after day end up as sand. The ebb and flow of water and waves grind them down. Lying in the sun and playing in the water will do that to a rock—and a person, too. A few weeks at the beach with nothing to do will recharge your batteries, but a few years on the beach will turn you to sand. God builds His Church on rocks, not sand.

Now think about how diamonds are made. They start as various minerals that by themselves are little more than garbage buried deep below Earth's surface. When these minerals come under pressure and are heated up, they become rocks. Increase the pressure, turn up the heat—literally to volcanic proportions—and give it a little more time, and you'll have a diamond. Something unbelievably valuable comes from something of relatively little value—if the screws are put to it. But look out! If during the process, the pressure is reduced, if the heat is turned down or if enough time does not pass, the rock will crumble and become the equivalent of sand. This is not scientifically exact, but it is close enough to make my point.

I was garbage until God saved me and made me a rock. Rocks are better than garbage, but they aren't diamonds. God is into making diamonds. And not only making them, but polishing and cutting and making perfect facets to reflect and refract His glory.

Once I am a diamond I can sparkle, but if I choose to run from pressure, turn down the heat or work according to my timetable instead of His, I will not become the gem He intends me to be. If I ever choose to give up or get out, life's ebbs and flows will reduce me to sand. Understand that sand isn't garbage. I'll never be garbage again. God made me a rock in Christ; sand is made up of rocks, but you can't build on sand.

Problems provide pressure and life is a lot like a furnace. Be a rock and endure while you are becoming a diamond. Just don't spend too much time at the beach.

–JC

Dear God, help me to see hard times as opportunities
for You to make me look more and more
like Your Son. Thank You. Amen

TODAY'S READING: 1 PETER 1:7; JAMES 1:2-8; ROMANS 5:1-8

An Eager Heart

Give thanks to the LORD and proclaim his greatness.
Let the whole world know what he has done.

PSALM 105:1

For a long time I defined "team spirit" as a willingness to lose oneself in the group for the good of the whole. I thought that was pretty good, but there was something lacking. It eventually dawned on me: If we are willing to do something, it doesn't necessarily mean we want to do it. We might do a task because someone asked us to or because everyone else is doing it. When that happens, it only means we want to please people.

On the other hand, if we eagerly want to do a task, our earnestness will show. We are going to work hard, take extra care and put in overtime. With this in mind, I changed my definition of "team spirit" from a "willingness" to an "eagerness" to lose oneself in the group. One word made a considerable difference.

The same idea applies to prayer. There is a big difference between a willingness to pray and an eagerness to pray. For me, it has never been a chore.

We are often willing to pray when we have a need but rarely when the going is good. I think we are too prone to magnify our problems. My father often quoted Abraham Lincoln as saying, "We'd all be much happier if we magnified our blessings rather than our disappointments."[1]

When we focus on what God has done for us, we will tend to be eager to thank Him. We will earnestly come to Him in all situations rather than just when we have a dilemma.

That does not mean that we cannot ask for help. We're all imperfect and we all have needs. The weak usually do not ask for help, so they stay weak. If we recognize that we are imperfect, we will ask for help and we will pray for the guidance necessary to bring positive results to whatever we are doing. It seems to me that when we give thanks along the way, we move from just being willing to come before God to being eager to do so.

–JW

Prayer does not have to be fancy or formal, but it can be. It is just as effective when it is simple and spontaneous. When offered seriously and sincerely, "Help!" or "Thanks" can be just as meaningful as the entire Lord's Prayer or an all-night prayer meeting.

Some prayer books and readings contain great prayers, and if they express what's on your heart, read them. Even prayers you once memorized and still know by rote can be good for today *if they are offered with the right attitude.* Virtually any prayer will do—if it comes from the heart and does not contradict God's Word.

It is the same with posture. Stand, sit, or prostrate yourself—it doesn't matter. Look up, look down, or close your eyes—do whatever helps you focus. Pray in the morning or before you go to bed. Shoot up "arrow prayers" during the day. They are all good if your heart is right. Raise your hands, clap your hands, or sit on your hands—you can praise God any way you want. King David even did it with dancing.

God is always listening. He wants to receive our praise and petitions, but He will only do so when it comes from our hearts. He isn't into us repeating words a thousand times just to fill time or carry on a tradition. He isn't impressed with us taking on a pious role just to act out a religious ceremony or to call attention to ourselves as the most spiritual in the room. Instead, He likes it when we come to Him willingly *and* eagerly as a child would in a healthy relationship with his or her father. We approach Him dependent, loving and adoring. He puts us on His lap and listens, wanting us to make requests, but He filters them with what is in our best interest and the best interest of the Kingdom.

How do we come to God with an eager heart? Seek His will and live with an eye toward heaven. Then ask Him to meet our needs. He knows what they are, but He wants a meeting of minds. In this way we say to Him that we are willing to lose ourselves for the good of His team.

–GC

Our Father in heaven, may Your name be honored.
May Your kingdom come soon. May Your will be done here on Earth, just
as it is in heaven. Give us our food for today, and forgive us our sins, just
as we have forgiven those who have sinned against us. And don't let us
yield to temptation, but deliver us from the evil one. Amen.

TODAY'S READING: PSALM 62:8; MATTHEW 6:7-13; ROMANS 12:12;
EPHESIANS 1:15-23; 6:10-20

A Good Habit

I have hidden your word in my heart, that I might not sin against you.

PSALM 119:11

I have always read the Bible. I did so as a youth. In college, I started virtually every day with a Bible reading. Nellie and I read the Scriptures together most evenings of our married lives. We read with our children when they were younger. I had learned the practice from my dad. I went to Sunday School regularly, both as a youth and as a collegian. I never stopped doing any of those things.

During my freshman year at Purdue, I learned that studying at night wasn't very productive. I lived in a fraternity house. Someone was always coming into the room. I started going to bed early and getting up at 3:30 A.M. to shower and study. There were no interruptions at that hour, and I could get done in a couple of hours what it would take four hours to do at other times. I began my study time with Bible reading.

I didn't read the Bible to please Mom, Dad or Nellie. It was a habit I enjoyed very much. I don't say that with any degree of pride. It was a habit of love, not one of requirement or drudgery. It wasn't just something to do, it was never a chore, and I enjoyed it.

–JW

Saint Augustine once said, "If you believe what you like in the Gospel and reject what you don't like, it is not the Gospel you believe, but yourself."[1]

The Bible is God-breathed and as such, every word has one perfect meaning, which conveys the thought God intended. Our goal is to determine what He wants to say to us. We cannot let relativity come into play when we study the Bible. There may be ten interpretations of what God said. That doesn't mean any of them are correct. God has one concept to convey.

We are to discover the meaning of a passage rather than give it one.

Bible study starts with studying the words. What these words mean and how they are used must be given priority. Interpretation is to be based upon the immediate and larger context. Always give preference to the clearest and most evident interpretation. Obscure passages must be interpreted in the light of clear passages.

Scripture may seem confusing at times, but it does not contradict itself. The Bible presents a unified message with accuracy and reliability. Everything essential is clearly revealed. We must not get hung up trying to figure everything out; rather, we must stand firm on the things we know. We should continue to ask questions and seek answers about the things we don't know. When we come across a passage we do not understand, we can do what Pastor Daniel Brown used to suggest during the Bible study he led years ago at UCLA: Put a question mark next to the unclear verse and continue reading. Chances are that when we come back to that passage, we will have learned more in the interim and it will now make sense.

Understanding God's Word was never meant to be impossible, but to understand it involves organized, consistent effort and a lifetime of commitment. When you are in your thirties or forties, you'll have all the answers. When you grow older, you'll have a lot more questions.

–*JC*

Heavenly Father, I want to hide Your Word
in my heart that I might not
sin against You. Amen.

TODAY'S READING: PSALM 119:9-16; PROVERBS 2:1-5; 2 TIMOTHY 3:14-17

Walking Your Talk

And you should follow my example, just as I follow Christ's.

1 CORINTHIANS 11:1

I began smoking during World War II. I would always quit during basketball season. I'd stop on my birthday in October and start again when the season ended. I never smoked in front of the boys. One of my reasons for finally quitting was to improve my example. I was convicted. I could no longer expect my players not to do what I was doing.

A leader's most powerful ally is his or her own example. There is hypocrisy to the phrase "Do as I say, not as I do." I refused to make demands on my boys that I wasn't willing to live out in my own life. Quitting smoking is just one example.

Leadership from a base of hypocrisy undermines respect, and if people don't respect you, they won't willingly follow you. One of my players complimented me greatly when he said, "Coach, you walked the talk."

At the beginning of each season I would give my players a letter. Part of it usually went something like this:

> Remember that you represent others who are responsible for you as well as yourself, and your personal appearance and conduct should not bring discredit in any way upon yourself or upon those whom you represent. Cleanliness, neatness, politeness and good manners are qualities that should be characteristic of those who are of great influence on young people, and you certainly qualify for that category. Be a good example.

–JW

Coach reminded his players that they were role models and that they had responsibilities to others. Mess-ups would reflect on each individual, the basketball program and the university. Each person was a part of something bigger than any one by themselves, and Coach wanted that "something bigger" represented well.

If we believe in God, we are on His team and He wants us to represent Him well. Just as Coach sent letters to his boys, God sent letters to us. His letters have been accumulated in a big notebook we call the Bible. God used the apostle Paul to write several of these letters. Today's passage is Paul's admonishment to believers at Corinth, where he had started a church. He wanted to be viewed as an example who pointed people to Jesus. He was also a leader who wanted them to be a similar example to others.

The example of leadership matters. We've all seen what good and bad examples in presidents can do to a country, and we've all witnessed what good and bad examples in evangelists and pastors can do to churches.

Although public figures such as politicians and church leaders may influence more people than you do, in your sphere of influence your example matters. Everyone looks up to someone and someone looks up to you. You probably have more sway with that person than does the president of the United States.

With this in mind, you cannot live with only your own well-being in mind. God has given you a responsibility to impact the people who watch you.

All too often, the only picture of Christ most of these people will ever see is on your face. This world needs godly role models. Therefore, not only your words but also your example need to be good ones. Be a constant and consistent example, a positive role model; and, to paraphrase Saint Francis of Assisi, "When necessary, use words."

–GC

Heavenly Father, help me to be a good
representative of Your Son in each situation
of every day and to each person
You bring my way. Amen.

TODAY'S READING: MATTHEW 5:16; ACTS 20:31-35; 1 CORINTHIANS 11:1; PHILIPPIANS 4:9; 1 THESSALONIANS 2:10-12; 1 TIMOTHY 4:12-16; 2 TIMOTHY 1:13; 1 PETER 3:15

Windows of Opportunity

*If you keep yourself pure, you will be a utensil God can use
for his purpose. Your life will be clean, and you will be ready for
the Master to use you for every good work.*

2 TIMOTHY 2:21

I must have the drive to develop my abilities and become the best I can be so that I'll be ready. If I'm prepared, perhaps my chance will come. But if I'm not primed, I'll miss my opportunity, and it isn't likely to come again. I have to think as if I'm only going to get one shot, so I must be ready.

It's true. There are some people whose chance is less likely to come. The circumstances of life are more difficult for them, and those circumstances may seem overwhelming. That's more reason to prepare and stay ready. Windows of opportunity are even more important to those people.

Consider Kenny Washington. He wasn't a starter in his sophomore or junior years at UCLA, but he was always ready whenever I used him in a game. For example, in two consecutive national championship games, he came off the bench and played a pivotal role. In 1964, against Duke, he scored almost thirty points. The next year, he rolled off almost twenty points against the University of Michigan. If he hadn't kept himself in a position to contribute and hadn't maintained a good attitude, he wouldn't have been able to answer the call the way he did. Because of his effort against Duke, he was on the cover of *Sports Illustrated*.

Doug McIntosh, in the same year and in the same game against Duke, came off the bench and played so well I kept him in for the rest of the game, and he started the next year. In 1965, Mike Lynn replaced Doug to finish out the championship game. Kenny, Doug and Mike are all good examples of players who were ready when their windows of opportunity came.

–JW

One of Coach's principles is to concentrate on what you do have, not on what you don't have. Having a positive attitude is the best way I know of to stay ready. Nobody did it better than Joseph. He wasn't the most humble when he was a youth, and he should have kept his conversations with God private, but he didn't deserve to be sold into slavery.

Joseph didn't let circumstances get him down. He stayed ready, got his shot and ended up running his new owner's household until the owner's wife went after him. Joseph, however, chose God's way, so Potiphar said "Bye-bye." Joseph actually went to jail for his stand. But he stayed ready, caught a break and ended up running the jail from the inside. Still, he stayed ready, caught another break and became second in command of Egypt.

The hand of God at work enabled the breaks to come Joseph's way. And God will do the same for you. But the point is that Joseph stayed ready and seized the moment when God opened a window of opportunity. Good old Joe didn't let his circumstances get him down. He looked at what he did have, not what he didn't have, and stayed ready. Joe's the kinda guy who would come off the bench and get you twenty or thirty points, if that's what it took to win the final game of the Final Four. He would have made Coach very proud.

God opens windows of opportunity for those who stay ready.

—*JC*

*Dear Lord, help me to do my part to stay pure
and filled with Your presence so that I'll be ready for the
windows of opportunity You open for me.
Thank You for giving me opportunities
to serve You. Amen.*

TODAY'S READING: GENESIS 37:3-5,20-21,27-28; 39:2-4,10,20-22; 41:14-15, 39-40; 50:18-20; GENESIS 37—50 (FOR THE WHOLE STORY OF JOSEPH)

Cake and Frosting

*Your heavenly Father already knows all your needs,
and he will give you all you need from day to day if you live for him
and make the Kingdom of God your primary concern.*

MATTHEW 6:32-33

When I played and when I coached, I always wanted to win. When I watch players compete nowadays, I see that over the years the desire to prevail hasn't changed. Athletes today want to win just as badly as the ones of any previous generation wanted to be champions.

Sure, today's players do more trash talking and show far less mutual respect, but this lack of consideration should not be mistaken for a shortage of desire. What has happened is that the emphasis has shifted from the Olympic spirit of competition for the sake of competition to winning and losing. Vast media coverage has helped this new attitude spread and grow. The desire to excel hasn't changed, but the focus on the outcome has.

Please do not misunderstand me. I wanted to win as much as anybody else. I'm fiercely competitive, so the games were important. However, the best competition I have is against myself—to become better. I did this with my teams, too. The competition was not so much against other teams as it was against ourselves—making us better. I knew if we improved, we would win more games, but winning was always the by-product of improvement. I wanted us to be the best we could be.

I felt that if we were fully prepared, we would do just fine. If we won, great—frosting on the cake. But at no time did I consider winning to be the cake. Winning has always been the frosting that made the cake a little tastier.

—JW

There are times when winning is paramount. World War II is an example. We had to win. Our freedom was at stake. Defeating communism was a big deal for the same reason. Terrorism threatens us now. We must prevail.

However, our culture has made winning at all costs and at all levels way too important, especially in sports. There is a vast difference between winning a war and winning a Little League game. John Wooden understood that distortion and kept a healthy perspective. Not all parents do.

A television commercial shows little kids playing Peewee League football. The quarterback throws a pass and slow-motion photography has us wondering if the receiver caught it. The announcer asks, "Did he make the catch?" The scene shifts to the kid and his dad having fun at McDonald's and the announcer answers, "Doesn't matter!" Time together is cake. Catching passes is frosting.

Mary sat at Jesus' feet, like a disciple, which was unheard of for a woman in that day. Martha grumbled in the kitchen. Mary spent a year's pay anointing Jesus' feet with costly perfume and tears. Judas griped about wasting money. Mary worshiped; the Pharisees worked. Mary knew cake when she saw it. Frosting distracted Martha and Judas, just as trying to earn God's favor by keeping rules distracted the Pharisees.

Jesus is the cake. Nothing else matters. The rest is frosting.

–GC

Heavenly Father, help me to focus on Jesus
and keep everything else in its
proper perspective. Amen.

TODAY'S READING: EXODUS 20:1-6; LUKE 10:38-42; JOHN 12:1-8

Everyone's a Teacher

So everywhere we go, we tell everyone about Christ. We warn them and teach them with all the wisdom God has given us, for we want to present them to God, perfect in their relationship to Christ.

C O L O S S I A N S   1 : 2 8

With the birth of my son in 1936, I was given a poster from the Grolier Society. On it was a picture of a man walking at the beach in the sand with a boy coming along behind, stretching out his steps as he tried to put his feet in the man's footprints. Inscribed on the poster was a poem by Lee Fisher, "A Little Fellow Follows Me." Its words have impacted me greatly over the years. Now I share them with you.

> A careful man I want to be,
> A little fellow follows me;
> I do not dare to go astray,
> For fear he'll go the self-same way.
>
> I cannot once escape his eyes,
> Whate'er he sees me do, he tries;
> Like me he says he's going to be,
> The little chap who follows me.
>
> He thinks that I am good and fine,
> Believes in every word of mine;
> The base in me he must not see,
> The little chap who follows me.
>
> I must remember as I go,
> Through summer's sun and winter's snow;
> I am building for the years to be
> That little chap who follows me.

The most important profession in the world is parenting. The second is teaching, and everyone is a teacher to someone.

–JW

Coach is a teacher, through and through. Neither age nor worn-out body parts have stopped him from practicing his calling. In his fabulous book *Be Quick but Don't Hurry*, Andy Hill tells a story about him sitting on the bench as a Bruin basketball player, becoming bitter and carrying his anger for more than twenty-five years. After entering the business world, Andy gradually came to see that his success was the direct result of what he had learned from Coach, even though he did not play much.

When Andy realized he had a fence to mend, he called Coach, who immediately invited him to visit. Andy went, not knowing what to expect. After hearing Andy's story, Coach smiled and said, "So you did learn something after all." With that Andy was able to release his anger, forgive and reconcile. He now has breakfast with Coach on a regular basis. Even in his nineties, Coach is ever the teacher, and on that day he taught forgiveness.

The Bible puts a great deal of importance on teaching. Although some people will be more gifted at it than others, we are all supposed to do it. Teaching is a skill that a follower of Christ should have. For example, we can't be called the Lord's servant if we are not prepared to teach effectively. Neither can we be an elder. The Bible clearly proclaims that every person must be ready to explain the hope he or she has in Christ.[1] Teachers fill such a vital need that the Word of God declares they are worthy of double honor.

I guess Coach is right. Next to parenting, teaching may be the most important role we can ever play.

–JC

> *Dear God, give me a passion to pass on*
> *what You've taught me. Give me opportunities*
> *and put people in my path.*
> *Help me to be a faithful teacher*
> *of Your Word. Thank You.*

TODAY'S READING: 1 TIMOTHY 3:2; 5:17; 2 TIMOTHY 2:2,24-26; COLOSSIANS 1:28

Getting in the Book

All who are victorious will be clothed in white. I will never erase their names from the Book of Life, but I will announce before my Father and his angels that they are mine.

REVELATION 3:5

Words have always been important to my family. My brothers all became English teachers, as did I. I suppose we got our love for language from our father. When we were growing up on the farm, every night he would read to us from the Scriptures and poetry. To this day, I usually read my Bible a couple of times a day, and I still enjoy attempting to express my feelings through poetry, especially when I'm feeling bluish. I love to read William Cullen Bryant, Longfellow, Poe, James Whitcomb Riley, Whitman and others.

I suppose I have written close to a hundred poems over the years, but most of them are for family and special occasions. I consider them private. My oldest granddaughter wrote a grade-school paper about her papa being a "good rhymer." I treasure that description and the memory of that moment.

I have also delighted in mentoring some of my players in the art of writing poetry. Over the years, these players and other friends have written and given me hundreds of compositions. I keep them in two books. The blue book is for the exceptional ones, but the ones in the other book are worthwhile as well.

Swen Nater, who played on my 1972 championship team, has written me more than one hundred poems. He is quite talented. All but one of his poems are in the blue book. Andy Hill, another former player, has penned three poems. They made the blue book, too.

I have poems from others who aren't as talented, but the thought is there, and they are just as meaningful to me as Swen's and Andy's. I appreciate the thoughtfulness behind them all.

—JW

Allow me to mix metaphors: The team photo is like the other book—every player gets in there—but not everyone makes the record book, which is like Coach's blue book. Coach hated the concept of starters and substitutes. All were a part of his team and he loved them equally, including the manager. But he knew that some players were more skilled than others and that only a few had All-American potential.

Now allow me to apply this illustration to make a spiritual point. All anyone has to do to make the team photo in the kingdom of God is trust Jesus Christ. However—and here is a twist—all of those who trust Christ who are willing to serve will make it into the record book, regardless of their ability. When it comes to playing the game of life for God, willingness is more important than ability or results. It is willingness to serve that makes a person an All-American in God's economy.

Who has shared Christ with the most people? Billy Graham comes to mind. He has preached a lot, but I'm thinking it was Handel. Millions of people listen to Handel's *Messiah* every year and folks have been listening to it since 1742. Yikes! If I have to compete against either of them to get in the record book, I'm sunk.

But here is some great news: I don't have to. Neither do you. If God gives us one person to talk to and we do it, we are just as successful in the Father's eyes as Billy is talking to millions. We're not competing against each other. We are just competing against ourselves.

If our motive is to be great, we never will be so in God's eyes. But if our motive is to serve, we can't help getting our names in the record book and becoming God's All-Americans.

The team photo and the record book are kept in the Book of Life. As long as our pictures are in there, we'll be okay. So make sure you're on the team. That's the first consideration. Second, approach life with a willingness to serve God, and the records will take care of themselves.

—GC

God in heaven, thank You for the role You have for me
in doing Your work in this world. Help me to reach my potential,
so I can fulfill the dreams You have for me. Thank You.

TODAY'S READING: REVELATION 3:5; 20:15; 1 CORINTHIANS 10:31;
JOHN 21:22; HEBREWS 11:1–12:2; MATTHEW 20:16

The legend at work: At UCLA, Wooden
became known simply as Coach.
Here he leads practice (above),
orchestrates a play (left) and guides
during a game (below left and right).

Plenty of pride: With cut-down nets and trophy in
hand, the Lew Alcindor-led Bruins celebrate winning
the 1967 NCAA basketball championship (above).
In 1972, following the seventh of a record ten championships, Wooden made the cover of *Sports Illustrated* as
Sportsman of the Year (center right). A few years later,
some of the all-time best UCLA players join Coach in
the locker room before an alumni game (below).

SAN FRANCISCO WINS THE WEST

Sports Illustrated

SPORTSMAN AND SPORTSWOMAN OF THE YEAR

COLLEGE
BASKETBALL'S
JOHN WOODEN

TENNIS
CHAMPION
BILLIE JEAN KING

Helping Others

You should remember the words of the Lord Jesus:
"It is more blessed to give than to receive."

ACTS 20:35

There is always great joy in learning that something you've said or done has been meaningful to another, especially when you do it without any thought of receiving anything in return. Your gift doesn't even have to be material. Helping others in any way—with a smile, a nod or a pat on the back—warms the heart. For many years I have quoted a poem. I don't remember who wrote it or where I got it, but it says a great deal about kindness:

> For you can't do a kindness without a reward,
> Not in silver nor gold but in joy from the Lord.[1]

I tried to get my basketball players to think that way on the floor, and I hoped it would translate off the floor, too. If a player scored off a pass, I wanted him to point to the man giving the assist until they made eye contact in a gesture of thanks and acknowledgment. I started that with my high school teams. I also wanted a gesture of thanks done for a good pick, for help on defense or for any other good play. Kindness makes for much better teamwork.

I don't believe a year ever went by when I didn't receive a letter from a custodian from one of the arenas where we played, indicating that we left the dressing room cleaner than anybody else. I wouldn't allow us to leave until the orange peels, gum wrappers, towels and soap chips were off the floor.

Jesus said, "It is more blessed to give than to receive." I've certainly found that to be true.

–*JW*

I am an only child and I fit the stereotype perfectly. Actually, I'm thrilled I didn't have siblings. I never had to share.

As a basketball player, I much preferred scoring to passing. If I had to be on a team, it would have to be a track squad or something like it, where I could compete in my event and then pool the score. Even after hoops, I wasn't much of a team player. I finally found my niche in life doing a one-man presentation.

But a funny thing happened on my way from the Forum (where I played pro ball for one year with the Lakers). After the NBA gig, God grabbed me, and nothing's been the same since. I'm still too *me* oriented; but, *oh my*, what changes have taken place since then. My thinking has been challenged and transformed.

I think one of the ultimate acts of selfishness and laziness is for a man to leave his urine in the urinal for someone else to flush, just because he doesn't want to touch the handle. I used to leave it. No more! I even catch myself picking up stray paper towels on the floor with the soiled ones in my hands. The custodian's got it rough enough as it is. That's all new for me.

My son remembers when I bought a stranded single mom a couple of new tires, so she could get where she was going. Such an act of kindness would never have occurred to me before.

I love letters in which the writer tells me someone received Christ after reading one of my books. Such good news means more to me than getting a check in the mail—unless it's a really big check. *Obviously, I still have a ways to go.*

Coach has had more time to get it right. He's over ninety years of age. But I'm learning that it really is better to give than it is to receive.

–*GC*

Father in heaven, You gave the ultimate gift to us.
Change me. Change my values.
Help me to love others more than myself. Amen.

TODAY'S READING: ACTS 20:35; GALATIANS 6:2; ROMANS 12:3

Talking Trash

Don't use foul or abusive language. Let everything you say
be good and helpful, so that your words will be an
encouragement to those who hear them.

EPHESIANS 4:29

When I was in the sixth or seventh grade, something happened that seems to be the singular event that has kept me from using profanity over the years. My older brothers and I were in the barn cleaning the horse stalls when one of my brothers threw horse manure in my face. I dropped my shovel, cursed and went after him. My dad stopped the fight right away, listened to our stories and then gave us both a good whipping. My brother got his for starting it. I got mine for using profanity—to this day, I still think mine was harder.

My dad never cursed and he wouldn't allow us to either.

Sometimes when I overheard one of my players use profanity during practice, I would dismiss him for the day. My boys all knew that practice was where they earned their playing time, so I used the sessions themselves as a disciplinary measure. If anyone cursed during a game, I would sit him on the bench for a while. It didn't take long for the players to clean up their language. There was no trash talk on my teams.

Once one of my players was asked if I ever used profanity. "Absolutely," he replied. "'Goodness, gracious, sakes alive' is profanity for Coach."

–JW

During my three years on staff with the Coach I never heard him use profanity, but everyone in practice knew he was at the end of his rope when he said, "Goodness, gracious, sakes alive!" That's as mad as he got. He controlled his mouth and expected everyone else to do the same.

The Bible has much to declare about wrong language: Don't use the Lord's name in vain, don't make oaths, and don't lie. It also makes clear that we are not to use corrupt talk.

"Corrupt" means rotten, decayed, foul, fetid, putrid, polluting and obscene. "Obscene" means being offensive to conventional standards of decency. But what's conventional? What's decent? What was objectionable yesterday is acceptable today. Relativism has taken its toll.

Athletes, construction workers, stand-up comedians and teenagers commonly use certain swear words, but those same words deeply offend many others. Regardless of how the profaner feels about decency, the use of four-letter words and the equivalent is coarse. Questioning someone's heritage is off base. It's wrong to make insinuations about anyone's mother. And calling a person driving an SUV an unprintable name is out of bounds.

What's the difference between profanity and firm speech? The apostle Paul walked a fine line. In Philippians 3:8, depending on the translation, he said that he counted everything that would keep him from knowing Jesus more intimately as garbage, trash or dung. In Paul's day what he said wasn't a swear word, but today's version that starts with the letter *s* clearly is.

In Romans 6:2, when someone wanted to keep sinning so that they could allow God to demonstrate more grace, the translators render Paul as saying, "May it never be," "God forbid," or "I should hope not."[1] But the Cotton Patch Gospels render the passage as "Hell no!" I'm not saying the s-word or the h-word are okay to use. God didn't put profanity in the Bible. But the apostle used the strongest cultural phrases possible, without being profane. So there is room for firm speech when the situation calls for it. For Coach that is "Goodness, gracious, sakes alive!" We shouldn't need anything stronger either.

–GC

Almighty God, help me to control my tongue. Forgive me for my past mess-ups. I want today to be a day when nothing unwholesome comes out of my mouth. Thank You. Amen.

TODAY'S READING: EXODUS 20:7; LEVITICUS 19:12; ECCLESIASTES 5:4-6; PSALM 39:1; MATTHEW 5:33-37; ROMANS 3:13; 6:1-2; PHILIPPIANS 3:8; EPHESIANS 4:29; JAMES 3:1-12

Color Blind

In Christ's family there can be no division into Jew and non-Jew,
slave and free, male and female. Among us you are all equal.
That is, we are all in a common relationship with Jesus Christ.

GALATIANS 3:28, *THE MESSAGE*

After I graduated from Purdue University, I coached high school basketball in Indiana. We had a good team and competed against other schools throughout the region. One day we were headed to Cincinnati for a game. However, the mother of one of the players did not want her son to go along because he would be competing against an African-American player on the opposing squad. This was before Martin Luther King, Jr.'s, speech, the March on Washington or any of the civil rights breakthroughs of the 1960s and since. But I instinctively knew what was right. Dad had helped set my thinking in place on the issue of race. Many times he told my brothers and me, "Don't consider yourself superior to anyone else, but never feel inferior."

I told the player's mother that if her son didn't play in Cincinnati, he wouldn't play in any other games either. She relented and he got in the game. When I coached at Indiana State University in 1946, we had a reserve who was black. When we won our league, we were invited to compete in the NAIA tournament in Kansas City, but tournament officials would not allow us to bring Clarence Walker. Again, I knew what was right, so we didn't go.

In these instances I wasn't really trying to make a political statement; I just wanted to do what was right. When you are a member of a team, you do everything as a team. One of my players once gave me a great compliment. He said, "Coach Wooden doesn't see race. He's just looking for players who will play together." Hearing that gave me about as good a feeling as I could ever have.

–JW

We're all prejudiced; we're not all racists. We all have built-in biases. Some we pick up from our families, others from our culture. This is a given. So the question is, Do we still feed, grow and exhibit our prejudices?

A few years ago, while talking to my African-American friend, the former UCLA basketball great Willie Naulls, I said something out of ignorance. Willie was candid: "Jay, that's the most racist statement I've ever heard you say." We'd been friends for thirty years. I paused, realized it was a hidden product of my past, repented and changed. Willie understood and accepted my apology, and the friendship grew. I have unseen prejudices that surface from time to time, but I'm not a racist. I want to change my thinking when I am wrong.

Words are powerful and they have different meanings for various people. The offense can come even when the genus of the word or phrase is not intentionally prejudicial. That's why I try to be careful. I don't keep a blacklist anymore. If saying "My finances are in the red" offends native Americans, I'll pick another color. I don't think people groups should be team mascots if members of the groups don't like it, regardless of tradition. Some traditions are prejudiced and ought to be changed. And I used to say, "It's a little nippy out," but I don't anymore—my son-in-law is of Asian descent.

During childhood every one of us developed prejudices. We are stuck with that. The question is what to do about them now. Do we perpetuate our hard-headed biases, let our intolerant attitudes affect our actions and become bigots? To quote a great man, "Goodness gracious sakes alive!" No! To do that would be wrong. Shouldn't we recognize our shortcomings and take steps to overcome them? Absolutely!

I hope you'll join Coach and me by committing yourself to eliminating your prejudices as each one is revealed to you. Remember what Coach's father said: "Don't consider yourself superior to anyone else, but never feel inferior."

–JC

Father, show me how painful it is for You
when I allow divisions among Your people.
Lord Jesus, You reconciled people of all backgrounds
to Yourself. Help me to do the same. Amen.

TODAY'S READING: ROMANS 10:11-13; EPHESIANS 4:13;
ROMANS 12:3-5; 1 CORINTHIANS 12:12-27

Buts and Promises

So when you make a promise to God, don't delay in following through, for God takes no pleasure in fools. Keep all the promises you make to him. It is better to say nothing than to promise something that you don't follow through on.

ECCLESIASTES 5:4-5

When I returned to Indiana after the war, I was somewhat disenchanted. Nellie and I had lost our home, and we were not sure what the future would hold. I turned down jobs at two very fine high schools and accepted a position at Indiana State University instead. I hoped that if I did well, I would have the opportunity to get a coaching job at a Big Ten school or perhaps another major university. I really wanted to go to my alma mater, Purdue University.

My Indiana State teams did very well, and after the second year, I got my break to move up. The University of Minnesota and UCLA had openings, and both schools offered me jobs. Minnesota seemed to be a good fit, and as a Midwesterner, it would keep me fairly close to home. I was ready to accept Minnesota's offer, but there was an issue we had to work out.

Minnesota's administrators were going to call me an hour before I was to give my final answer to UCLA. That way I would know whether the Minnesota situation was an option. I never received a call. I didn't know it, but a snowstorm had knocked out the lines. Therefore, when UCLA's representative called, I accepted. The Minnesota people got through to me an hour later and said all the details had been resolved. I thanked them for the offer but told them I could not take it. I was sorry, but I wouldn't break my word to UCLA.

I came to UCLA not as a first choice. I came because a college teammate, who now was on the UCLA football coaching staff, thought that there would be a future there. I came because there was a snowstorm and Minnesota's people could not get through to me. And I came because I had given my word.

–JW

A British pastor once used the following three-point outline for a message he delivered to an audience in America:

1. Everyone has a *but*.
2. Everyone else's *but* looks bigger than yours.
3. You can see someone else's *but* better than you can see your own.

I'm told the Brits don't use the word "butt" much, but it sure does make the pastor's outline funny in the colonies. He wondered why everyone laughed so much. After I chuckled at the cultural connotations and thought about it, I agreed with him. Everyone has a but. But it's the big ones that keep us from keeping our promises.

Coach Wooden could have said to UCLA, "But the snowstorm messed up the call," "But it's only been an hour" or "But I'd rather take the Minnesota job." But Coach didn't let his buts become big.

Early on, when I didn't know what my ministry calling would be, I thought about missions—but I hate bugs. Later, when God directed me to a support-based ministry, I had another big but. I thought, *But, God, I don't want to have to be dependent on others for money.* God used a wonderful couple that gave my wife and me a big check to get us started. It took a big sign to overcome my big but. But it shouldn't have been necessary. My faith was too small and my but was too large.

A guy who talked to Jesus had a big but. He even made a promise: "I will follow you, *but* first let me say good-bye to my family."[1] He wanted to wait until it was more convenient. His but kept him from following and keeping his promise. I know people who have promised to serve God that are waiting until they achieve financial security or reach retirement. Still others are waiting until the kids are grown.

"Later's," "until's," "if's" and "when's" are really nothing more than buts. Don't let yours keep you from keeping your promises. Coach didn't.

–*JC*

Father God, give me the courage
and the character to do what I say I'll do.
Thank You, Lord, for keeping Your promises.
Help me to keep mine. Amen.

TODAY'S READING: GENESIS 3:12; ECCLESIASTES 5:4-5;
MATTHEW 8:18-22; LUKE 14:16-24

Discovering Your Knack

Observe people who are good at their work—skilled workers are always in demand and admired; they don't take a back seat to anyone.

PROVERBS 22:29, *THE MESSAGE*

Do not permit what you cannot do to interfere with what you can do. This is one of the most important tenets by which I have lived my life.

We tend to get too concerned about events over which we have no control. We spend time thinking about the negatives, and that time could be much better spent focused on things over which we have control. Spending time on what we can't control has an adverse effect on what we can control and on what we should be doing.

When I came to UCLA, I was led to believe that by the end of my three-year contract I would have a facility in which we could play. I must be honest. They never promised me a new building, but it was a mutual expectation.

For years my teams practiced in the old barn. Before we could practice, I had to sweep the floor to get rid of the dirt from the physical education classes that were also held in the building. We played our games around town in whatever venue was available. We never had a home-court advantage. But I didn't allow myself to get too down about it, although I wondered how much we could accomplish under these conditions.

Eventually we did accomplish a lot. We even won our first two national championships under these conditions. I'm sure that if I hadn't gotten over my negative feelings, that would never have happened. Thankfully, I was able to eventually get myself to focus on what we could do. I worked with what I had, and I didn't dwell on the things over which I didn't have control.

Jay Carty calls this knowing your knack.

–JW

I haven't always known my knack. For example, I spent eleven years in management. I learned on the job and was actually pretty good at it, but it is not what I was naturally wired to do. Learning like this will ultimately make a person wake up in the middle of the night screaming, regardless of how good they are. It costs too much energy.

When I left the business world and got into ministry, I took a management position. It was what I knew but still not what I was wired to do. That led to more screaming in the night. When I finally mustered up the courage to validate my speaking talent, my whole world changed. I discovered and developed my knack. I became what the Bible calls wise.

There are eight Hebrew words that translate to mean "wisdom" or "wise." The primary word is *chokmah* (chauk´-mah) and it's used 146 times in the Bible. It literally means "know-how," or "knack."[1] Solomon noted the importance of knowing your knack and developing it. I've substituted "your knack" or "their knack" for the word "wisdom" and "prudent" for the word "wise" in the following quote from Proverbs 1:1-7:

> The proverbs of Solomon the son of David, king of Israel: to know *your knack* and instruction, to discern the sayings of understanding, to receive instruction in *prudent* behavior, righteousness, justice and equity; to give *prudence* to the naive, to the youth knowledge and discretion, a man who *knows his knack* will hear and increase in learning, and a man of understanding will acquire *prudent* counsel, understand a proverb and a figure, the words of the wise and their riddles. The fear of the LORD is the beginning of knowledge; fools despise their *knack* and instruction (*NASB*, emphasis added).

In this passage, "wisdom" means the wise ones are those who develop their God-given talents and become skillful. In Exodus 31:3-6, we read that God has given us knowledge, wisdom and skill in specific areas. Here is an overlooked concept: Gain knowledge and become wise by developing your God-given know-how, or knack.

God has not gifted us to do all things well. With this in mind, we should not permit what we cannot do to interfere with what we can do. In other words, God wants us to discover our God-given wiring and develop it.

–GC

Heavenly Father, show me my knack so that I can develop what I can do to be the best I can be for Your honor and glory. Yes!

TODAY'S READING: PROVERBS 1:1-7; 22:29; EXODUS 28:3; 31:3-6

Things That Last

Not that I was ever in need, for I have learned how to get along happily whether I have much or little. I know how to live on almost nothing or with everything. I have learned the secret of living in every situation, whether it is with a full stomach or empty, with plenty or little.

PHILIPPIANS 4:11-12

We are all equal in that we can all strive to become the best we are capable of becoming. We can always improve, but we shouldn't compare ourselves to others. We get in trouble when we start trying to measure up to someone else.

Generally speaking, we measure ourselves by people who have more of something we want—usually material things. That's not a positive approach at all. Often those with considerable wealth don't have the lasting things in life such as peace and contentment. Often they aren't as happy as many who have far less. When it comes to wealth, it's very difficult to handle too much and it's also very difficult to handle too little. It's better to be in the middle. Some material assets are not important, and others are essential, of course.

Everyone wants to do as much as he or she can for his or her family. However, if a person gets too focused on material things, he or she will forget the more lasting things. All material assets, in one way or another, will go away. I really believe that happiness comes from things that cannot be taken away from you.

I never have had substantial material goals, and I'm so glad my dear Nellie wasn't set on material things either. We never lived in a mansion or drove the fanciest of cars, but we were happy and had enough. And we always appreciated the things that last—especially faith, family and friends.

—JW

It was good that the apostle Paul knew how to focus on things that last, because he suffered greatly. He worked hard, was put in jail often, was whipped times without number and faced death again and again. Five times he got thirty-nine lashes. Three times he was beaten with rods. Once he was stoned. Three times he was shipwrecked. Once he spent a whole night and a day adrift at sea. He traveled and faced numerous dangers from the elements, robbers and other adversaries. He suffered weariness, pain, sleeplessness, hunger, thirst and cold. And he had the pressures of telling people the truth about God and starting new churches. He wasn't always happy, but he learned to be content. He lived out his words, "I can do all things through Him who strengthens me."[1]

King Solomon learned a similar lesson. He had tried it all, including the party scene, alcohol, drugs, women, material things and other bad stuff. He had status and power, yet he despaired. He hated life. But he chose to straighten up and fly right when he concluded: "Fear God and obey his commands, for this is the duty of every person."[2]

Paul had nothing, yet he was content because God was his priority. Solomon had everything, yet he was miserable until God became his priority. I think if I were miserable, I'd choose to be rich and miserable over poor and miserable; but I must ask the question, Why be miserable? If we want contentment, we must pursue God, not things, and take the measure He gives without comparing what He gives us to what He gives to someone else.

–JC

Father, I want to find contentment in You and You alone.
Show me if I have any priorities other than You.
Thank You, Lord.

TODAY'S READING: PHILIPPIANS 4:10-13; 2 CORINTHIANS 11:16-28;
ECCLESIASTES 1:16–2:23; 12:13-14

Reminders and Idols

So commit yourselves completely to these words of mine. Tie them to your hands as a reminder, and wear them on your forehead.

DEUTERONOMY 11:18

In 1943 a friend gave me a small cross and I've carried it in a pocket ever since. It's not a good luck charm, or anything like that, but I held it in my hand during games and I still grab it during times of tension. It reminds me who is in control and who I represent. It probably is a good thing for officials that I had that in my hand when a bad call was made. Although the phrase was not in vogue back then, in a way the cross in my pocket spoke to me and asked "What would Jesus do?" in any particular situation.

My cross is pretty worn, but I still carry it today. I do not have to grab it nearly as often as I once did, but it comforts me to know I still have the reminder. Some years back, another friend sent me a poem that best describes my association with the little cross:

I carry a cross in my pocket, a simple reminder to me
Of the fact that I am a Christian no matter where I may be;
This little cross is not magic, nor is it a good luck charm.
It isn't meant to protect me from every physical harm.
It's not for identification for all the world to see.
It simply is an understanding between my Savior and me.
When I put my hand in my pocket to bring out a coin or a key,
The cross is there to remind me of the price He paid for me.
It reminds me, too, to be thankful for my blessings day by day
And to strive to serve Him better in all that I do and say.
It's also a daily reminder of the peace and comfort I share
With all who know my Master and give themselves to His care.

So, I carry a cross in my pocket, reminding me, no one but me,
That Jesus Christ is the Lord of my life if only I'll let Him be.[1]

—JW

Many years ago, I was speaking at my home church on a Sunday night and afterward gave away stickers that read "WHAT WOULD CHRIST DO IN THIS SITUATION?" I instructed people to put the stickers where they needed them the most. The following Sunday night I asked where the stickers went. People put them on refrigerators, desks, notebooks, televisions, dashboards, inside purses and just about everywhere imaginable.

Clearly, I was ahead of my time. A few years ago someone put "WWJD" on a cloth bracelet and gave away millions. "WWJD" is a prompter to ask "What would Jesus do?" A lot of people use the WWJD bracelets as genuine reminders, but to others the bracelets are nothing more than jewelry or good luck charms. Coach does not wear a bracelet, but he has his cross and it clearly points him toward the Savior.

While God gave reminders to His people, He also warned against perverting them and turning them into idols. Anything can become an idol when we place it ahead of God or attribute to it powers that only God has. A bronze snake on a stick that cured poisonous bites later had to be destroyed because people started worshiping it. The Old Testament recounts how God had people wear little sacks that contained reminder verses. But by New Testament times, Pharisees wore them as jewelry and to let everyone know that they were religious big shots. Then there was the girl who wanted a necklace, so she went into a jewelry store and asked for one of those crosses with that little guy on it. She had no idea what it stood for.

When we look around us, we can see all sorts of symbols. Some point us toward God, some have become objects of worship, and others have been reduced to items of jewelry. When we see a religious icon, we should never let it become anything more or less than a reminder.

–*GC*

Dear God, will You remind me when I'm about to mess up?
I want to stop sinning against You. Help me to increase my time between
mess-ups and decrease my confession time. Thank You.

TODAY'S READING: NUMBERS 21:4-9; 2 KINGS 18:4;
DEUTERONOMY 11:18-21; MATTHEW 23:27-28

Praying to Win

Oh, that you would bless me and extend my lands! Please be with me in all that I do, and keep me from all trouble and pain!

1 CHRONICLES 4:10

In 1942, Frank E. Davidson, the man who gave me the cross I carry in my pocket, operated an interfaith men's club called The Forum. It was held during the Sunday School hour. Men would attend and then leave to worship at their own churches.

I was to receive a fifty-two week faithful attendance pen. The night before, we had won the finals in the sectional tournament against a Catholic team. Their coach, Johnny Howe, also attended the men's club. That morning Frank said, "There I was at the game last night and here was Johnny Wooden, who I knew was going to receive his medal for not having missed in the last year, and there was Johnny Howe with his team all blessing themselves. Now wasn't our Lord in a helluva spot?"

I never encouraged anyone to pray for a win. I don't think our prayers should be directed to the score of a game. That seems way too selfish. I wanted my boys to honor God by doing their best, controlling their emotions and asking for protection. Those are good requests for basketball players and for our lives in general.

When counseling my players who had problems off the court, I also recommended prayer. I always told them I was sure God hears all of our prayers and answers them—but sometimes the answer is no.

–JW

A few years ago Bruce Wilkinson wrote a book titled *The Prayer of Jabez*. It was a *New York Times* best-seller and millions of copies were printed. It's about a guy who prayed to be a winner, but he didn't pray for a win.

In 1 Chronicles we find a long list of names. If you have never read the Bible, don't start here unless you want to name a new baby something weird. There is a hiccup in the listing at 4:9-10. Then it goes back to listing names until chapter 10. Jabez is the hiccup. He gets two verses—one for him and one for his prayer and God's answer.

All we know about Jabez is that he "was more honorable"[1] than his brothers and that it must have been very painful for his mom when he was born. That's it. The rest of the Bible is silent about him.

Jabez asked for God's blessing, wider borders, God's constant presence and freedom from fear and pain. God said, "You got it!" The inference is that Jabez got it because he was honorable and that he wanted wider borders to expand God's influence, not his own. God gave Jabez all that he asked for, including as much wealth as he could handle without causing him to stumble.

Jabez wanted everything God had for him, asked for it and got it. Notice that Jabez didn't want more than his neighbor. He wasn't trying to beat anyone and he didn't ask for God's blessing at someone else's expense. He didn't pray for a win, but he wanted to be a winner.

Don't pray to win. Such a request is not biblical. Instead, be a winner by being honorable and staying satisfied with asking for the fullness of God's blessing, presence, influence and protection—for His glory, not yours.

–*JC*

Oh, that You would bless me and extend my lands!
Please be with me in all that I do,
and keep me from all trouble and pain!
I ask this for Your glory, not mine. Thank You.

God's Hall of Fame

For the LORD sees every heart and understands and knows
every plan and thought. If you seek him, you will find him.
But if you forsake him, he will reject you forever.

1 CHRONICLES 28:9

I like Walt Huntley's poem "God's Hall of Fame." I first heard this adaptation of it at a Fellowship of Christian Athletes Conference in Estes Park, Colorado, in 1964. Here is the part that speaks to me most:

> This crowd on earth
> They soon forget
> The heroes of the past.
> They cheer like mad
> Until you fall
> And that's how long you last.
> But God does not forget
> And in his Hall of Fame
> By just believing in his Son
> Inscribed you'll find your name.
>
> I tell you, friends, I would not trade
> My name however small
> Inscribed up there
> Beyond the stars
> In that celestial hall
> For any famous name on earth
> Or glory that they share.
> I'd rather be an unknown here
> And have my name up there.

Losing my wife Nellie was the hardest thing in my life, but I am confident I will be with her again because our names are written "there beyond the stars." Christ was in the center of her life, as He is in mine.

–JW

My computer is a Mac. As far as I'm concerned, Windows 95 turned a PC into a 1987 Macintosh and PCs have been playing catch up ever since. The Mac contains an old software program called Scrapbook. It is a place to keep handy snippets of text or pictures for future use. When I was writing my book *Playing with Fire*, I came across a piece of text I didn't realize was there. I didn't remember putting it in my Scrapbook file. I don't even remember having read it before, so I don't know the author and I don't know the source (if you wrote it, please contact me and I will credit you when this book is reprinted). It will inspire everyone and remind Christians of what we value. However, it is perfect for the person who is considering whether or not to ask Jesus Christ into his or her life and in so doing have his or her name "inscribed up there beyond the stars in that celestial hall."

What does your life revolve around? Remember this as you consider your answer. We have made ourselves the center of everything in this world. But God will be at the center of everything in heaven. The decision you made or will make, either for or against Christ, should be measurable by what your life revolves around. If it's not God, you won't like heaven, and you probably won't get to go there.[1]

Where is Jesus in your life? Outside? Inside but relegated to the bench by your other priorities? Or is He on the throne of your life? As you think about this, consider 1 Chronicles 28:9:

And Solomon, my son, get to know the God of your ancestors. Worship and serve him with your whole heart and with a willing mind. For the LORD sees every heart and understands and knows every plan and thought. If you seek him, you will find him. But if you forsake him, he will reject you forever.

–*GC*

Lord Jesus, I want my life to revolve around You and I want You to be in complete control. I want to know that my name is recorded in heaven. Thank You. Amen

Love and Trust

Amos Alonzo Stagg, the famous football coach, has influenced me greatly. He emphasized the role of love and the importance of doing what is best for each player.

Coach Stagg admitted that he didn't admire all of his players, but he did love them. He wanted love to dominate his coaching career. He also stressed that getting the most from his players would be the outcome of doing what's best for them.

Each year before our first practice I would tell my players something like this:

I will love you all the same, but I won't like you all the same. You won't like each other all the same; you won't all like me the same. I understand that.

You may feel, at times, that I have double standards, as I certainly will not treat you all the same. I think treating everyone the same shows partiality. However, I will attempt to give each player the treatment that he earns and deserves according to my judgment and in keeping with what I consider to be in the best interest of the team.

—JW

Coach didn't give this speech to his players to motivate them; rather, he did it to teach them. Motivators appeal to emotions. Coach didn't like the ups and downs that come with that approach. He was into proper preparation, which eliminates peaks and valleys.

Coach's way of relating to his players worked. No wonder—it is also the way God identifies with us. Coach was simply following the example set out in the Bible. He had authority during practices and games. The players could submit or not. If they submitted, they were part of the team and contributed as their abilities allowed them to and according to the roles Coach assigned. If they didn't submit, they were dismissed from practice, sat on the bench during the games or left the program.

Likewise—only on a much grander scale—when we submit to God, we get to enjoy a bond that those who won't submit miss. Plus, we get to participate in matters of eternal consequence, according to our gifts, abilities and the sphere of influence God entrusts to us. God loves us all the same and proved it when Jesus Christ died. Salvation is available to everyone who believes.

However, God does not treat us all the same. Once our eternal destiny is determined by faith, He will continue to shape us so that we progressively look more and more like Jesus. Since no two people are alike, it takes different strokes for different folks to see this happen. God will also take into account our individual abilities, gifts, roles, attitudes and track records. It is interesting to note that God usually entrusts a lot to a person only after he or she has been faithful with a little.

Whatever our treatment, we can be certain that God loves each of us the same and always has our best interests in mind. All we have to do is submit.

–JC

*Heavenly Father, I want to bring glory to Your name
through the living of my life. Make me all You want me to be.
Lord, thank You that I can trust You to be loving and
compassionate. I trust You with my soul. Amen.*

TODAY'S READING: PSALMS 40:9; 143:7-11; ROMANS 12:1-2; HEBREWS 13:20-21

Building a Shelter

Yes, a person is a fool to store up earthly wealth but not have
a rich relationship with God.

LUKE 12:21

Too often, we think of a shelter against a rainy day as a roof over our heads, a retirement portfolio, a savings account or, at the least, our social security payments. But material things will all disappear. The Old Testament character Job said something about coming into the world naked and leaving it the same way.[1] Indeed, the Bible says we won't be taking anything with us.

There is a wonderful axiom about the three things most people really want out of life: happiness, freedom and peace of mind. Interestingly, these things are usually attained when we give them away. When we are fortunate enough to have them, the three are also a form of shelter. The life we lead and the friends we make can be shelters, too.

My dad talked about the need to build a shelter, but he never told me what kind of shelter he was talking about. He left that for me to discover. But he pointed me in the right direction.

I don't think my dad was talking about any form of earthly shelter when he told us to build one against a rainy day. I think he was referring to a more lasting shelter. Specifically, I think he was talking about ensuring a place in heaven.

Of course, through Christ, I have built that shelter.

–JW

My dad was a Depression kid. Business came easily to him and he retired at forty-nine. As he got older, I remember him joking, "If I can't take it with me, I'm not going!"

My dad, as I have noted elsewhere, received Christ when he was in his eighties, three weeks before he died. He almost trusted in the wrong shelter. He wanted to pack a bag for eternity, but in the end, he could not. Like all of us, he came into the world naked and left the same way.

My mom had a close call, too. She was an alcoholic who became a street person, giving herself away for a place to sleep at night. It was as ugly as your mind can conceive.

She came for a weekend visit when she was sixty-four. I was married by then. Mom knew I would search her bags because booze was not allowed. That's why she rarely came. I had to work that day, and Mary, my dear wife, spent the day talking to Mom about Jesus. When I walked through the door, my mother met me and asked if I would pray with her. She said, "I would like to receive Christ. Would you pray with me?" I got to lead my mom to the Lord!

Her life changed. She stopped drinking, got a job and an apartment, met a guy and remarried. She died three years later. She came with nothing and left with nothing, but, like my dad, she built the right shelter—just in time.

It's been an interesting journey for me. My wife and I risked everything when we started Yes! Ministries. Mary said, "It feels like we're jumping out of an airplane and putting on a parachute on the way down." Yet God blessed our meager beginning. I've since spoken to hundreds of thousands of people in person, through my books and on radio and television. For thirty years, I've had the privilege of helping people build shelters.

It's been a great way to spend my life. I didn't make a lot of money, but I have no regrets. I arrived naked; I'll be leaving the same way because I won't be taking anything with me. But I won't need anything because, like Coach, I've got a shelter waiting.

–*JC*

Dear heavenly Father, thank You for telling me about Jesus,
the most important shelter of all.

TODAY'S READING: MATTHEW 6:19-34; JOHN 14:1-3; JOB 1:21;
1 TIMOTHY 6:7; PSALM 20:6-8

Getting to the Point

Consider it all joy, my brethren, when you encounter various trials,
knowing that the testing of your faith produces endurance.
And let endurance have its perfect result, that you may be perfect
and complete, lacking in nothing.

JAMES 1:2-4, NASB

A coach ought to be interested in people and their welfare. Such an interest best comes from a foundation of spirituality. People in my profession have a priceless entrustment. I had to deal with young men who were under tremendous stress physically, mentally and emotionally. I had to be strong.

In my book *They Call Me Coach,* I paraphrased something that I had read or heard from another coach:

> The coach who is committed to the Christlike life will be helping youngsters under his supervision to develop wholesome disciplines of body, mind and spirit that will build character worthy of his Master's calling. He must set the proper example by work and by deed. It is not easy.[1]

Without spiritual strength I'm not sure how good of a job I could have done. I'm certain my teaching would have suffered.

I have defined success elsewhere in this book, but allow me to do it again. This is my life's most defining maxim: Success is peace of mind as a direct result of self-satisfaction in knowing that you did your best to become the best that you are capable of becoming—in all areas of life. It is very difficult to be successful without a strong sense of spiritual well-being. I believe God wants us to be strong in our faith. Jesus said to seek Him first and then He would add all things.[2] I have sought Him first and foremost, and I have tried to do my best. I am at peace.

In a nutshell: To be a success, seek Him and do your best.

–JW

A four-year-old child was learning to look both ways before going out into the road. One day there was a freshly hit, dead squirrel, with guts and everything spread out, right in front of where the little girl was about to step off the curb. Her dad said, "Oh, that's too bad. I'll bet a car was going too fast."

"Maybe," said the child, "but the squirrel didn't look both ways."

She got it! The little girl fully understood what happens when we don't check to be sure the road is clear. Dad had missed the point.

People everywhere know about John Wooden's notoriety as a basketball coach, but the ten championships in twelve years and all the wins don't really define the man. His outward success is the product of his inward philosophy. Coach Wooden spent fourteen years developing his Pyramid of Success. Like the girl and the squirrel scenario, Dad may see the championships and the win-loss record but miss the point. We need to be like the little girl and grasp his philosophy.

There are twenty-five qualities in Coach's pyramid. I want to focus today on the two at the top. We won't be successful unless we have faith and patience.

> What is faith? It is the confident assurance that what we hope for is going to happen. It is the evidence of things we cannot yet see.[3]

Faith provides inner strength. God's rewards are the ones that matter—not those from people—so faith is crucial to success.[4]

Patience is the other major component, and in a nutshell, it means we need to learn to wait under pressure. A synonym for "patience" in the Bible is "endurance."[5] Within the concept of success, you can't experience it if you aren't willing to endure. But you will get it all if you'll learn to wait.

What's the point? Seek Him and do your best. You will be a success. But you'd better learn to endure along the way. Good things take time.

–GC

Almighty God, give me faith, teach me patience,
and fill me with the desire to glorify You
in all that I do. Thank You, Lord. Amen.

TODAY'S READING: JAMES 1:2-4; HEBREWS 10:32-39; 11:1,6; 12:1-3; ROMANS 3:21-28

Going Beyond Good Intentions

The LORD your God will delight in you if you obey his voice and keep the commands and laws written in this Book of the Law, and if you turn to the LORD your God with all your heart and soul.

DEUTERONOMY 30:10

There have been times in my life when I meant well, but I didn't follow up or follow through when I should have. My intentions were honorable, but my actions did not match my intentions.

There have been times when I should have called a sick friend or someone who had suffered something tragic. I knew I should act, but I didn't. There have also been times when I have put off the letter I should write. Sometimes it never gets done. I know the smallest good deed is better than the best intention. Lots of people talk it, but they don't walk it. While I have often fallen short, I have always tried to act upon my intentions.

Since retiring, I do things because I want to, for the most part. Before, I did a good deal because I had to. It didn't necessarily mean I wanted to, but certain acts were expected of me. I eventually realized that I am going to do the best at the things I want to do, so when I retired, I negotiated out of my life some of the things I don't like or want to do. Not all, but some.

Come to think of it, if I only did what I wanted to do, I would not be obedient to the creator. Sometimes He wants us to do certain things that we may not feel like doing. When it comes to what God asks of us, we need more than good intentions—we need to follow through fully.

–JW

Jesus had cleaned house in the Temple the day before. The chief priests controlled the sale of sacrifices and they lost a lot of money. When the Son of God came back to town the next day, the power players—religious leaders, chief priests, scribes, elders, Pharisees and the like—confronted Him. These guys were hearers and memorizers of the Word of God, not doers. They worshiped to be seen by people, they prayed to be heard by people, and their goal was to maintain power over people. Jesus was a threat to their power bases.

"By what authority are You doing these things?" they demanded.[1] They were trying to trap Him.

But Jesus turned the tables on them with a parable about a father who asked his two sons to go to work in the vineyard. One said he would and didn't. The other said he wouldn't and did. Then Jesus asked, "Which of the two did the will of his father?"[2] The leaders agreed: It was the son who changed his mind and did his father's will.

In basketball terms, Jesus gave the religious guys a facial when he made it clear they were like the first son: All show, but no go.

Five frogs were on a log and three decided to jump. How many are left? We don't know. Saying they're going to jump doesn't mean they jumped. What matters is how many actually jumped.

We are to be doers of the Word of God, not hearers only. And we need to be doers for the right reasons. I was born in Missouri. We would say "Show me"—as that is the state slogan. If we were in a Nike commercial, we would say "Just do it."

—GC

Father, may my behavior prove me to be a doer of Your Word. Don't let me delude myself by being a hearer only, and don't let me settle for good intentions. Amen.

TODAY'S READING: MATTHEW 21:23-32; JAMES 1:19-27; 2:14-26; PHILIPPIANS 4:9

Real Progress

*Prove by the way you live that you have really turned
from your sins and turned to God.*

MATTHEW 3 : 8

Although there is no progress without change, not all change is progress. I think young people want to be different, but being different doesn't necessarily mean progress. As a rule, youth have lots of ideas, but they want to make too many changes. When we get older, however, we tend to become content with the status quo and we forget that there is no progress without change.

I used a low-post offense for six years when I had seven-foot centers Lew Alcindor and Bill Walton on my teams. But for the other thirty-four years, I had shorter teams and used the high-post offense. Within both systems I made changes and variations. We won national championships with strong forwards and we won with strong guards. And, of course, we also won championships when we had our two fine centers. In each case, I adjusted the offense accordingly, because there is no progress without change.

When I coached in high school, I taught the two-hand underhand free throw. I still believe it is the best way to shoot them. But I changed when I coached in college because the players hadn't been brought up shooting them that way.

Personally, it took me two years of grieving before I was ready to get on with my life after losing my wife, Nellie. I had to change and move on. Also, I've been fairly private about my faith over the years. This book is evidence of change in that area, too. Even at ninety-two there is no progress without change.

–JW

When I'm out to eat with families that have kids, I usually get everyone to do what I humorously call a sin check. Then I'll stick a spoon to my nose and say, "See, there's no sin in my life. The spoon wouldn't hang there if there was." I tell everyone that they can't eat until they hang a spoon from their noses. Kids get into it right away. Cool teenagers are reluctant. Adults rarely will try. It is a fun way to pass the time before the food arrives.

There is a trick to hanging a spoon from your nose. When no one is looking, wipe your nose off with a napkin. You have to remove the body oil. Then do a "haaaa" on the spoon, like you do when you moisten your sunglasses before cleaning them. Finally, place the spoon on your nose, and it will stay.

Why can't repentance be that easy? Well, it is! But let's face it: People sin because they want to do their thing, not God's thing. If sin weren't fun, nobody would do it.

It's easy to get little kids to repent though. I think that's why Jesus wants us to come to Him as if we were children. Kids easily approach their heavenly Father as Abba. That means "Daddy." Actually, it's "Abba Father," or "Daddy, Daddy." It's a tender term.

You can get too cool or "adult" with me, and refuse to spoon hang before we eat, but don't try that with God. You can fold your arms and suck on prune pits and stare me down if you want, but that does not work with God. Be like a child. Humble yourself. Spoon-hang for Jesus. Turn from sin to God. That's what repentance is. It means you have to change, and there is no progress without it.

—JC

Lord God, I don't think I'm good enough to
be with You apart from Jesus, and I don't want to
behave in ways that aren't pleasing to You.
Father, forgive me of my sins and
help me change my ways.

TODAY'S READING: MATTHEW 3:2; 4:17; MARK 6:12; LUKE 5:32; 24:47;
ACTS 3:19; 20:21; ROMANS 2:4

Looking Down

For through the grace given to me I say to every man among you not to think more highly of himself than he ought to think; but to think so as to have sound judgment, as God has allotted to each a measure of faith.

ROMANS 12:3, *NASB*

Too often, it seems that when an individual receives unusual praise or acclaim, it has an effect on them. I didn't want to be changed by any honor or success that came my way, so I went about my playing and coaching in a way that I would not be fazed by praise or criticism. I wanted my players to do the same.

I always told them that they would receive criticism, both deserved and undeserved. I made it clear that they would not like either one. I also prepped them to receive praise, both deserved and undeserved. I stated the obvious—that they would like that very much. Then I did what I like to do best. I taught them a lesson. I said that their individual strength of character would shape how they reacted to both praise and criticism. If they let either one affect them, it would affect them adversely.

When a person changes, he or she usually ends up with a feeling of superiority. I didn't want that to happen to my players and I didn't want it to happen to me. I was flattered when one of the coaches at the NCAA convention introduced me by saying, "John is no different after winning ten championships than before he won one." That made me feel good because I want to practice what I teach.

I hope I haven't changed. I don't ever want to look down on anyone.

–JW

It is so easy to get uppity and full of ourselves. It is healthy to have people around us who will bring us back down to Earth. As it is written in Proverbs 27:6, the wounds of a friend really are better than the kisses of an enemy. To show you what I mean, let me tell you a few stories, each of which stresses the importance of humility, not superiority.

A seminary student was taking his last final exam. The final question was worth 50 percent of his grade. "What is the name of the dorm custodian?" The young man was enraged and confronted his professor. The professor looked up and spoke gently, "Jesus showed compassion for, and interest in, those who occupied the lower stations in life. If you are going to represent Jesus properly, the custodian is the first person you should have met. For four years, she has cleaned your room, scrubbed your toilet and emptied your trash. You have had four years to learn her name. Until she becomes of interest to you as a person, you don't qualify to be a pastor."[1]

When reunions are held for players from Coach Wooden's years at UCLA, managers are included. They are considered an integral part of the team. In some basketball programs, a manager becomes a gofer to the all-stars on the squad. Not at UCLA! They are equals, and that is as it should be. It's the Wooden way.

Pharisees in Jesus' day could be overheard praying, "Thank You, Lord, that You have not made me a Gentile, a dog or a woman." Jesus had good news for Gentiles and women. He set them free. That God didn't play favorites was a brand-new idea. That a person's station in life shouldn't make any difference as to how each was treated was radical thinking. In Christ's eyes, we are all equal.

Don't look down on people from whatever height you climb. Make sure you always look at them eye to eye.

–GC

Dear Lord my God, help me to reflect Your love
to everyone You place in my path today.
May there be no exceptions. Amen.

TODAY'S READING: MARK 9:33-37; ROMANS 12:3-8; GALATIANS 3:28

Jay Carty in action: His Oregon State Beavers (above left and right) were good but not good enough to beat Wooden's Bruins in the NCAA playoffs. In 1966, Carty was a UCLA freshman team coach (below), specifically assigned to tutor future Hall-of-Famer Lew Alcindor.

Just short of the ring: In 1969, Carty spent one year playing for the Los Angeles Lakers, a team that fell one game short of winning the NBA championship.

Being Thankful

*No matter what happens, always be thankful, for this is
God's will for you who belong to Christ Jesus.*

1 THESSALONIANS 5:18

As I grow older I appreciate things that I didn't appreciate much when I was younger. I am thankful more than I used to be. I've been reasonably healthy, and I feel blessed. And each morning I can think, *This is going to be a good day!*

I don't ever think, *Why did this happen to me?* I'm just thankful for what I have. Too often we're not thankful enough.

I enjoy my memories. I have more and more of them. However, there are fewer and fewer people with whom I can share them. I remember silent movies, but I don't have many people left in my life who actually went to see them. I've seen so many changes in my days.

I've been blessed with grandchildren and great-grandchildren who live close by, and I get to play with them. They have helped keep me thinking young. In fact, being associated with younger people for most of my life has helped me to stay active. Continuing to fly to events and be a part of things such as the Wooden Classic and the Wooden Award has helped me stay connected.

Many, perhaps most, of my former players are close to me. Rarely will a day go by when I won't talk to at least two or three of them. Sometimes I will have breakfast with them. It's been helpful to me to have those relationships. For this, I am very thankful.

–JW

I ran a Christian camp in the mountains east of Los Angeles. It was there that I learned a very valuable lesson in thankfulness.

In the summer we brought in as many as fifty high school and college students to work on the staff. It was hard work at low pay, but the results were eternal. Two-thirds of the way into summer was always the toughest time of year. By then, people had grown tired and were on edge. They would begin to shift their focus from the task at hand to what they would be doing in the fall.

One year was particularly tough. The entire staff was at the end of its rope. It was then that one of the kids remembered a concept I had taught at devotions earlier in the summer. At a staff meeting he said, "Jay, we've just about had it, but there are still three weeks to go. We need a count-it-all-joy party."

The *King James Version* of the Bible renders the beginning of the book of James with the words: "Count it all joy when ye fall into divers temptations."[1] King James English is tough. The New Living Translation is easier: "Whenever trouble comes your way, let it be an opportunity for joy. For when your faith is tested, your endurance has a chance to grow. So let it grow, for when your endurance is fully developed, you will be strong in character and ready for anything."[2]

The idea is that God cares so much about us that He wants to perfect us, and He does it by testing our faith so that our endurance will grow. So what we did that particularly tough summer was throw a big party, complete with cake, hats, horns and poppers that shot streamers. We celebrated the fact that we had never been so tired in our lives. Then we thanked God for caring so much for us that He would turn us into toast, even though there were three more weeks still left. We thanked Him for what we were still going to learn.

Our thankful attitude got us through the last three weeks and taught us valuable lessons that continue to impact our lives today.

–*JC*

Father God, thank You for caring enough about me to help me be
of strong character and ready for anything. I thank You for
saving me through Jesus Christ. I thank You for the plans
You have for me. I thank You for all things. Amen.

TODAY'S READING: COLOSSIANS 3:23; JAMES 1:2-4; 1 THESSALONIANS 5:18;
1 CHRONICLES 16:8; PSALM 100:4

Riding the Pine

At the time, discipline isn't much fun. It always feels like it's going against the grain. Later, of course, it pays off handsomely, for it's the well trained who find themselves mature in their relationship with God.

HEBREWS 12:11, *THE MESSAGE*

Walt Hazzard was a great passer and a fine floor leader, and he understood what I wanted to do, but he tended to be flashy when it wasn't necessary. It wasn't easy to get Walt to give up some of his playground habits.

Early in his sophomore year, I benched him against the University of Colorado, and we lost. The next night I benched him against Colorado State, and we lost in double overtime.

I gave him three choices: play the game my way, sit and not play, or go someplace else. He decided to quit and called his dad to tell him. His dad talked him out of it. Walt stayed and became one of the best ball handlers I ever coached. His sophomore year, in the semifinals of the Final Four, we lost by two points to the eventual NCAA champions. In his senior year (1964), he was a consensus All-American and played an integral part in our first NCAA championship.

I found the bench to be the greatest ally I had to make individuals comply with what was best for the team. As a result, we lost a few games but developed character in the lives of many young men. We won more championships than any other team ever has, but more important, we developed champions on and off the court.

–JW

Coach Wooden knew the difference between punishment and discipline. Punishment is for the punisher's benefit—to make him or her feel better. Discipline always has the other person's best interest in mind. Coach never physically punished his players. They never ran laps or did push-ups for mess-ups. He wanted them to discipline themselves, but when they didn't or wouldn't, he dismissed them from practice or used the bench (riding the pine) as his molding tool, even at the cost of losing a few games. There is nothing like the pine to shape behinds and wills.

For God, there is also a difference between punishment and discipline. To understand clearly, we need to first see why God even allows us to mess up. He could have made us as robots that mechanically have to say "I love you." But He didn't. God isn't into robots. Instead, He wants us to want to say it and show it. That means we have a choice between loving and serving God or not. If we don't, we've messed up. If we mess up as a Christian, we may find ourselves riding God's pine. We must then decide if we want to play, sit or leave the program. If we mess up by not choosing to follow God at all, we may find that we are not even on the team.

When we get right down to it, heaven is the reward for choosing God's program. Hell is the consequence for playing the game of life our way. Keep in mind that God doesn't send anyone to either place. He just made the rules. We do the sending by making choices to either believe Him or not.

The ultimate goal of God's discipline is to help us make choices that are in our best interests. We should never think God is punishing us for something we've done. That's not His style. But He will use the circumstances and consequences of life to mold and shape us—this is called discipline. Just like Coach did with his players, God would rather we discipline ourselves, but He will do it if He has to.

Take it from me. It's a lot easier to discipline yourself than to have God do it for you. When you do it yourself, you don't lose any playing time.

–GC

Heavenly Father, You say in Your Word that there is a way that may seem right to me, but the result is separation from You. God, I repent from wanting to do things my way. Discipline me when necessary that I might make choices that are pleasing to You. Amen.

TODAY'S READING: HEBREWS 12:4-13; 1 CORINTHIANS 9:24-27; PROVERBS 12:1; 15:10; 23:12; REVELATION 3:19

The Placement of Pats

You can't antagonize people and then expect to get positive results. I never punished players by making them run laps or do push-ups. I withheld privileges. Discipline was maintained through denying practice time or playing time in games. I don't believe physical punishment is helpful. I didn't want physical conditioning confused with punishment. Early on I made the mistake of antagonizing through physical punishment. I learned a better way, and as a result, I became a better teacher.

I always started practice on time, but I didn't always stop on time. I learned it was just as important to stop on time as it was to begin on time. When I did that, I got more out of the players. Organizing practices and having precise beginning and ending times allowed us to get more done with the time we had. It ceased being necessary to keep players longer, and they quit pacing themselves because of an unknown finishing time.

While I may have occasionally raised my voice, I never yelled at players much. That would have been artificial stimulation, which doesn't last very long. I think it's like love and passion. Passion won't last as long as love. When you are dependent on passion, you need more and more of it to make it work. It's the same with yelling.

Some of my players needed a pat on the back. For others, the pat needed to be a little lower and a little firmer.

–JW

In the previous chapter, we looked at how God uses the bench to build character, break rebellious wills and teach patience before He puts us back into the game. But we didn't delve into who got benched. If you've ever spent time on the sidelines, you're in very good company.

Moses was raised by Pharaoh's daughter and was being groomed to play a role in the headman's court. But Moses had a problem with anger, and when he killed an Egyptian with a single blow, God sent Moses to the bench for forty years. Afterward, the time with his derriere in the chair had prepared him to lead his people out of Egypt.

Jonah hated Assyrians, but God wanted him to go to Nineveh and tell 'em to turn or burn. Jonah wanted them to burn, so he took off in the other direction. There was a storm at sea; he got thrown overboard, swallowed by a fish and barfed onto the shore. That's a lousy way to travel and a worse way to arrive. Then God put Jonah's smushed tush on the sidelines to watch his shade wither on a hot day. After cooling his jets for three days in a stinky stomach and who knows how long watching a worm gobble his cover, God put him back in the game.

Even King David got his pride bent on the sidelines. He had to run from Saul, hide in a cave, drool in his beard and pretend to be Looney Tunes before God let him get the slivers out of his rump.

Abraham spent time on the pine, Jacob spent fourteen years waiting on a woman, and the apostle Paul spent nine years on the sidelines before God let him rock the world.

God won't yell at you when you mess up. He'll even pat you on the back if you keep trying. But if you don't repent, he'll pat you a little lower and a little firmer, and you'll find yourself on the sidelines. How long you stay there is determined by the time it takes you to repent and how much you have to learn.

–GC

Heavenly Father, help me to lengthen my time
between stumbles and decrease my confession time.
I want to stay in the game and finish well to
bring glory to Your name. Amen.

TODAY'S READING: JONAH 1:1—4:11

Criticism and Correction

Fathers, don't aggravate your children. If you do,
they will become discouraged and quit trying.

COLOSSIANS 3:21

Criticism and correction differ, especially when it comes to methods and motives. Criticism puts someone down. Correction means I want to help.

Be slow to correct and quick to commend. No one likes correction, but we learn from it. If we commend before we correct, the person will accept the correction better. But we must listen before we correct. There is usually another side to every story. If we listen to others, they will be more apt to listen to us.

It is very important how correction is given. We must be careful how we do it. We don't want those being corrected to lose face. Here are some good tips: Make it meaningful, but use judgment. Don't fly off the handle and be quick to correct. Do it with tact. If we just let fly, it is more likely to be viewed as criticism than as correction.

A leader must analyze carefully all of the people under his or her supervision, specifically recognizing the fact that no two people are identical. Two people may be alike in many respects, but what motivates one won't necessarily motivate another. There are no set formulas that will work with everyone. The goal is to bring out the best in each person, knowing in advance that the approach you as a leader take and the results with each person will be different.

Approval is a greater motivator than disapproval, but we have to disapprove on occasion when we correct. It's necessary. I only make corrections after I have proved to the individual that I highly value them. If they know we care for them, our correction won't be seen as a judgment. I also try to never make it personal.

–JW

We have already looked at punishment and discipline. Today, we are focusing on criticism and correction.

Like punishment, criticism is punitive. The primary beneficiary is the giver, not the recipient. Criticism provides the giver an excuse to be angry and an object on which to focus his or her wrath. For the few who benefit from this style of coaching, there is a wake of bruised and battered young people who should have been protected.

The concept of constructive criticism with children is an oxymoron. It is irresponsible for parents to allow Little League coaches to scream and browbeat kids, regardless of so-called successful won-loss records. If a high school graduate chooses a Bobby Knight type to be his or her college coach, that's one thing; but in our schools or clubs, prior to college, there is no place for coaches who humiliate young people. When children don't have a choice, they shouldn't have to be exposed to continual caustic criticism.

Like discipline—but unlike criticism—correction always focuses on the best interests of the recipient. It leaves a child with his or her dignity. It doesn't crush the spirit. Substitute the word "correction" for "love" in the following Bible verse to get an idea of how correction ought to occur:

> Love is patient and kind. Love is not jealous or boastful or proud or rude. Love does not demand its own way. Love is not irritable, and it keeps no record of when it has been wronged. It is never glad about injustice but rejoices whenever the truth wins out. Love never gives up, never loses faith, is always hopeful, and endures through every circumstance.[1]

What about correction and firmness? Correction can be firm. Believe me, "Goodness, gracious, sakes alive" was unbelievably firm when Coach prefaced his comments with those words. But it was never followed by harshness, a demeaning attitude or belittling methodologies.

Sometimes it's necessary for parents to be lovingly firm when correcting, but there is no room for a critical spirit or an angry or humiliating vocabulary. Parents should start with correction, move to discipline, and punish only as a last resort. But never, never, never use criticism.

–JC

Heavenly Father, I desire to put away my critical spirit. Help me to be loving when I'm called to correct. Thank You, Lord. Amen.

TODAY'S READING: 2 TIMOTHY 3:14-17; 1 CORINTHIANS 13:4-7;

PROVERBS 15:1-2; COLOSSIANS 3:21

Going to the Stands

They said, "You Galileans!—why do you just stand here looking up at an empty sky? This very Jesus who was taken up from among you to heaven will come as certainly—and mysteriously—as he left."

ACTS 1:11, *THE MESSAGE*

I was a student of coaching and talked to as many coaches as I could. When Frank Leahy took the Notre Dame football job, he allowed me to attend one of his practices. I learned a lot from him. His practice organization was highly detailed, and mine became more that way after observing him.

I loved preparing for practice. Every day the staff and I would meet for a couple of hours to carefully plan. The meetings began at 10:00 A.M. We would schedule each minute and every aspect of the practice. I wanted the team manager to know how many balls we required and where and when we would require them. We evaluated who needed extra work and on what. I enjoyed scheduling the drills that would make us better. All coaches and managers had minute-by-minute details and instructions written on three-by-five cards. For years, I kept a record of every practice session in a loose-leaf notebook. That way I could refer to it in the future.

I loved working with my boys and I loved practices. Since retiring, I don't miss the games. I miss the preparation for the games. I liked to think that we were so well prepared that once the game started, I could go up in the stands and the team wouldn't miss me.

–JW

Jesus was a stickler for details, too. For three and a half years, He ran the practices and His disciples were His boys. Then, on the Thursday night before the biggest event in history, He had His last meal with His staff. The next day He would take the sins of the world on His shoulders, conquer death a couple of days later, coach His team for forty more days and then go into the stands to watch the rest of the game.

Jesus had already told them that He would only be with them "a while longer."[1] The disciples didn't get it. They didn't understand when Jesus stilled the storm on the Sea of Galilee, they didn't get it when it was time to heal people and cast out demons, and they didn't get it in the Upper Room. The disciples just flat out didn't have much of a clue. They needed a helper.

Passover required a spotless sacrifice. Jesus qualified, offered himself and was killed. But when He conquered death a few days later, He couldn't stay long. God could only touch a few people in the confines of a body. Even if He had CNN, He couldn't reach them all. But He could through the Holy Spirit, whom Jesus called the Helper.

In the Upper Room, Jesus took the time to prepare His men for the happening of the Helper, even though He knew they wouldn't get it, at least not until the Spirit arrived seven weeks later. Only then would they understand the drills Jesus had run during practice and why He went into the stands to watch.

–*gc*

Dear God, thank You for sending the comforting
presence of Your Holy Spirit who guides me.
My desire is to listen carefully to what You have to say
and to willingly do Your will. May it be so.

TODAY'S READING: JOHN 16:1-15; ACTS 2:1-4

Looking Back

I'm not saying that I have this all together, that I have it made.
But I am well on my way, reaching out for Christ, who has so
wondrously reached out for me. Friends, don't get me wrong:
By no means do I count myself an expert in all of this, but I've got my
eye on the goal, where God is beckoning us onward—to Jesus.
I'm off and running, and I'm not turning back.

PHILIPPIANS 3:12-14, *THE MESSAGE*

I love poetry. Today I want to share with you a poem that I wrote a number of years ago. I hope it speaks to you as its meaning has spoken to me.

Do Not Look Back
The years have left their imprint on my hands and on my face,
Erect no longer is my walk and slower is my pace;
But there is no fear within my heart because I'm growing old,
I only wish I had more time to further serve my Lord.

When I've gone to Him in prayer, He has brought me inner peace,
And soon my cares and worries and all other troubles cease,
He has blest me in so many ways; He has never let me down,
Why should I fear the future when I soon may touch His crown?

Though I know down here my time is short, there is endless time
   up there,
And He will forgive and keep me forever in His loving care,
May I not waste an hour that's left to glorify the name,
Of the one who died, that we might live, and for our sins took all
   the blame.

—JW

The advice columnist Ann Landers once reported, "The number one problem above all others seems to be fear."[1] A doctor estimates that 90 percent of all chronic patients had fear as their first symptom.[2] Current problems such as pollution, terrorism, political intrigue and the constant threat of war in the Middle East and North Korea make a person yearn for Franklin Roosevelt's good old days when "the only thing we [had] to fear [was] fear itself." We live in a scary world.

Coach had a scare awhile back. His office chair broke and he spilled forward, wedging himself against the coffee table. With the weight of the chair on him and the table limiting his movement, he didn't have the strength to move. He was trapped for more than three hours until his son-in-law came by because his daughter couldn't reach him on the phone. With his bad hip and two bad knees I'd think he would be fearful, but he was not.

How many ninety-two-year-olds do you know? How many ninety-two-year-olds do you know who fix their own meals and still drive a car? I don't know about you, but my answer is one. John Wooden prefers being independent, and he's not afraid of being alone.

At one time death scared him. No more though. He hopes he dies before any more of his loved ones do, but he's not anxious about it. It's a preference. Coach isn't caught up in fear, like so many of us are. He's looking forward. He's not fearfully looking back over his shoulder.

Inscribed across an old map of Jamaica is the title "Land of Look Behind." The map goes back to the days when there were slaves in Jamaica. When the slaves escaped, they headed for the mountains. The government would send troops after them, so the slaves frequently looked fearfully over their shoulders. This gave the mountainous area the name Land of Look Behind.[3] Coach Wooden doesn't live there anymore. His relationship with God has taken him past that.

–JC

Heavenly Father, I want my head to stay forward
and my eyes looking up. Forgive me when I let the circumstances
of life take my eyes off You and look backward in fear. Amen.

TODAY'S READING: PSALMS 91; 23:4; 27:1-3; 46:1-2; PROVERBS 29:25;
JOHN 14:27; 2 TIMOTHY 1:7

After You've Learned It All

Moses called all the people of Israel together and said,
"Listen carefully to all the laws and regulations I am giving you today.
Learn them and be sure to obey them!"

DEUTERONOMY 5:1

I prefer to call myself a teacher rather than a coach. I am also a learner. In fact, I like to think that during my last year of teaching (coaching), I was a better teacher than I was the year before.

I tried to improve each year. Of course, the growth curve is greater at the beginning. I learned more my first year of teaching than any other single year. I didn't show as much progress in the latter years, of course, but I always continued to learn. In fact, even after retiring, I have refused to stand still, and I'm into my nineties.

If I am ever through learning, I am through. You either have to go forward or you'll go backward. You rarely move rapidly upward, but you can go downward very fast.

I'm a visual learner. I do better when I'm able to see something. I had cataract surgery a few years ago. Now my eyes tire and I have to use a magnifying glass. It's inconvenient. The result is decreased reading time, and I feel like I'm missing out on a lot. I'm definitely not getting as much done as I once did, but I'm still trying to discover new things. There are poems I want to memorize and books I want to read.

I believe you ought to learn as if you're going to live forever, but you ought to live as if you're going to die tomorrow. If I've learned anything in my ninety-plus years, I have come to understand that it's what you learn after you know it all that really matters.

–JW

Moses told the Israelites to listen, learn and obey. Listening is absorbing and accepting information. Learning is understanding the meaning and implications of what has been taught. Obeying is putting into action all that has been absorbed and understood. Coach would add another thought: He believes the final law of learning is repetition. Absorbing and understanding something over and over again make action instinctive.

There are so many ways to apply this in our lives. I like the idea of the repetition of righteousness. We'd learn a lot more and sin a lot less if we repeated righteous acts.

A story has been told about Socrates holding a young wanna-be's head underwater and later asking him, "When you were under the water, what was the one thing you wanted more than anything else?"

"I wanted air."

Then Socrates said, "When you want knowledge and understanding as badly as you wanted air, you won't have to ask anyone to give it to you."[1]

King David was as thirsty for God as that young man was passionate for air: "O God, you are my God; I earnestly search for you. My soul thirsts for you; my whole body longs for you in this parched and weary land where there is no water."[2]

What would life be like if you were to have the same thirst for God that David had? You would learn all you could about your heavenly Father, wouldn't you? As your relationship grew more intense, you would keep discovering new truths and experiencing new intimacies. And just about the time you thought you had learned it all, I guarantee it would be then that He would teach you His deepest truths—the ones that matter the most. It's the way He works. So passionately pursue Him and enjoy the journey.

–JC

Almighty God, I commit myself to reading
and listening to Your Word. I ask You to help me
understand it through the power of
the Holy Spirit. Fill me with the desire to
learn and to obey. Amen.

TODAY'S READING: PSALMS 42:2; 143:6; PROVERBS 12:1; 15:31-32; 23:12

Real Trophies

When you bow down before the Lord and admit your dependence on him,
he will lift you up and give you honor.

JAMES 4:10

I was glad when we won our sixth NCAA championship in 1970. I finally got a watch for myself. The previous five went to my son, my son-in-law and my three grandsons. I have since given one to my doctor and one to my dentist.

My son, Jim, was dearer to me than the watch, so he got the first one. They were men's watches, so giving one to my son-in-law was like giving one to my daughter, Nan. And it is obvious why my grandsons got theirs.

Of all the awards I've received, the one I cherish the most is the Big Ten Medal for Academic Achievement given to the graduating athlete with a high grade point average. I got that in my last year at Purdue. The one I am second proudest of is the Bellarmine Medal of Excellence because a previous recipient had been Mother Teresa, the person who has lived in my lifetime for whom I have the greatest respect. Nellie put both of them on the wall in my den.

Both were nice to win, but I'm not tied to the trophies. I've cleaned some out over the years. My family members will be coming over soon to take the rest of what they would like to keep. Except for the Big Ten medal, the Bellarmine medal, my first watch and the Presidential Medal of Freedom, I'll probably get rid of the rest. Again, my ties are not to trophies. My ties are to my family and to my former players. They are the real trophies in my life, and that is why I have included some pictures of them in this book.

–JW

When Coach talks about his trophies and how people are more important to him, it humbles me and reminds me what a humble man he is. It also reminds me of a character I once created for my book *O. Whillikers in the Hall of Champions*. Please allow me to digress today (I will be back on track tomorrow) and explain by telling a little bit of Hugh Mills's story—a dreadful pun, I know, but cut me some slack. It's a fun way to make a great point.

His majesty Karl Kingfish the Great was the grandest grouper in the grotto. He presented the marlin Hugh Mills with an award at a banquet one night. "Hugh," he said, "I'd like to present you with this shiny gold medal. I'll read what it says: "To the most humble citizen in Kingfish County." And that's not all. Our local university, Fish U, named a word after you and put it in the dictionary. It's Humility . . . a Hugh Mills word.

Hugh Mills thought about putting on the medal and strutting in front of the other fish. But he didn't. If he had, I guess the others would have had to take it off of him because Hugh wouldn't have been Kingfish County's most humble citizen any more. Instead, he put the medal on his wall where he could see and enjoy it. He didn't flash it at the town fish because he didn't want them to feel put down or envious. You see Hugh Mills really was a humble marlin.[1]

Many winners in life will be losers in God's economy, and many so-called losers will be winners with God. True humility and fear of the Lord lead to riches, honor and long life. Put your trophies on the wall or give them away. Humble yourself under the mighty power of God, and in His good time, He will honor you.

–*JC*

Dear God, forgive me for thinking more highly
of myself than I should. And forgive me for those times
I thought I might be good enough to stand
in Your presence apart from Christ. Amen.

TODAY'S READING: PHILIPPIANS 2:1-11; 1 PETER 5:6-7; JAMES 1:21;
PROVERBS 15:33; 18:12; 22:4; MATTHEW 19:30

Playing the Odds

Some nations boast of their armies and weapons,
but we boast in the LORD our God.

PSALM 20:7

I've been asked, "Isn't it better to be the underdog?"

No, I don't want to be the underdog. Would you rather fight someone who has whipped you twice or someone you have whipped twice? There is no question in my mind. It's not even close. If it's a fight, I want to fight the guy I've already whipped twice. Coaches aren't being honest with themselves when they say they'd rather be the underdog. I'd much rather be the favorite.

Players would sometimes say, "Coach, it seems like everyone is pointing for us. Everybody gets up for us."

I'd reply, "Let's keep it that way. Isn't that the way we want it? They are honoring us when they do that. I hope it always stays that way."

When you come onto the floor with confidence, not cockiness, and the other team has used emotion to prepare to defeat you, you have a tremendous advantage. Your first run will deflate whatever has been pumped up; your relentless confidence will usually prevail. I wanted my players to be extremely confident in their preparation and in their ability to do their best. I don't think we ever expected to lose a game. A loss was always a real surprise. I suppose that's why losses were so rare.

No, it isn't better to be the underdog. The race doesn't always go to the fast and the strong, but it's a big surprise when it doesn't. The favorite wins most of the time. That's how it got to be the favorite.

–JW

My dad was a bookie. He mostly took bets on horse racing and football games, but you could get a bet down on most anything if you wanted to. The people who set the odds don't get everything right, but they know enough about what they do to get it right more than the person on the street. You might beat them occasionally but not over time.

It's the same with the lottery. Paybacks vary, but a typical return is fifty cents on every dollar spent. Do the math! We can't beat the odds unless we hit the big one—and the odds of doing that are usually around 14 million to one.

I also learned a lot about gambling from my dad. One of the biggest lessons was don't risk very much on long shots or the underdog. Those rarely come through.

I'm opposed to wagering, but let's face it, life is a gamble. Why not play the best odds you can get? I know, a lot of people do not like the concept of playing the odds. Instead, we call it decision making. I am easy on that point. If you do not like the word "odds," call it "probabilities."

You have to bet your soul on something. Here are your choices: Atheists believe there is no God. New Agers believe they keep going around until they get it right. Agnostics are betting God grades on the curve. Universalists believe everyone goes to heaven, no matter what. The relativist believes we create our own reality. Christians believe Jesus Christ is the way.

Which one is right? We can't say they all are. Jesus said they aren't. So if any of the others are right, Jesus was wrong.

What are the odds of the basic truths of the Bible being wrong? Consider that it has never been proven wrong archeologically or historically. Some prophecies haven't been fulfilled yet, but no event in history has ever contradicted biblical prophecy. There were over sixty specific prophecies made four hundred to fifteen hundred years before Jesus Christ was born that were fulfilled by Him.

Which of the options have the best odds of being true? While you're deciding, remember you are not betting money or even your life; you have to bet your eternal soul. Coach and I believe the accuracy of the Bible makes Jesus the odds-on favorite.

–*GC*

Dear Lord, thank You that I can walk confidently with You today, knowing that my soul is secure in Jesus Christ. Amen.

TODAY'S READING: JOHN 13:36–14:24

Encounters of the Best Kind

*Jesus said, "'Love the Lord your God with all your passion and prayer
and intelligence.' This is the most important, the first on any list.
But there is a second to set alongside it: 'Love others as well as you love
yourself.' These two commands are pegs; everything in God's Law
and the Prophets hangs from them."*

MATTHEW 22:37-40, *THE MESSAGE*

Abou Ben Adhem (may his tribe increase!)
Awoke one night from a deep dream of peace,
And saw, within the moonlight of his room,
Making it rich like a lily in bloom,
An angel writing in a book of gold.
Exceeding peace had made Ben Adhem bold,
And to the presence in the room he said,
"What writest thou?" The Vision raised its head,
And, with a look made of all sweet accord,
Answered, "The names of those who love the Lord."
"And is mine one?" said Abou. "Nay, not so,"
Replied the Angel. Abou spoke more low,
But cheerily still, and said, "I pray thee, then,
write me as one that loves his fellow men."

The angel wrote and vanished. The next night
It came again with a great wakening light,
And showed the names whom love of God had blessed,
And lo! Ben Adhem's name led all the rest.

The first time I read this poem, written by James Henry Leigh Hunt, it
struck me. This was a spiritual encounter of some kind. I sat back and envi-
sioned a book of gold and the question, "What writest thou?" Then it hit
me: Love your fellow man. It's the second commandment. I know we are to
love God first, but we must also not forget to love each other.

–JW

Jesus summarized the Ten Commandments in two directives: love God and love people. Love God is first—this makes it so we can't emphasize the second commandment over the first and get away with it. If we reverse the order, our neighbor becomes an idol, and God will have none of those before Him.

If the poet were trying to say that all we have to do to be approved by God is love our fellow man, he'd be contradicting Scripture. Who is God in flesh? Jesus! According to the first commandment, whom must we love to love God the way He wants to be loved? Jesus! We must never take Jesus out of the equation.

However, if the poet is saying that we can determine how much we love God by how much we love people, then he got it right. Jesus asked Peter three times, "Do you love me?"

Peter said, the equivalent of "Yes" each time.

Three times Jesus told him what that kind of love ought to look like when he said, "Take care of my sheep."[1]

If we don't love people, how can we love God? Indeed, we are to love God and to love people, but we must not love people more than we love God. These are important concepts. God made sure Coach got them right. Take a moment to ponder these thoughts. He wants you to get it right, too.

–JC

Oh, God, deepen my love for You and Your people.
Show me how to tend to Your sheep.
In Jesus' name, I pray.

TODAY'S READING: MATTHEW 22:37-40; JOHN 21:15-17; 1 JOHN 4:7-11; 1 CORINTHIANS 13:1-13

Spoiled Rotten

Brothers and sisters, we urge you to warn those who are lazy.
Encourage those who are timid. Take tender care of those who are weak.
Be patient with everyone.

1 THESSALONIANS 5:14

The worst thing you can do for the ones you love are the things they could and should do for themselves. I think Lincoln said that first—I'm not sure—but I've used it so much over the years that the saying has become a part of me. I've used it a lot because I deeply believe it.

I'm convinced we do too much for others, and I think it has hurt our nation. I know it has hurt our society and our families. When you do too much, neither countries nor people appreciate it. If people are hungry, give them fish. But after they have eaten, teach them how to fish. Don't keep giving them fish. That makes them dependent on you for their food. It's never good to take away anyone's independence.

I coached my players not to expect time-outs during games, and I didn't want them looking over at the bench for directions. Once the game started, I didn't want them to need me.

Coaches tend to do too much for their players. We get summer jobs for them, so they don't learn how to get jobs. We give them too much help with their studies, so they don't learn how to learn. If we directed them in how to do things rather than doing things for them, they would be a lot better off.

It's the same with our children. We tend to spoil them by overindulging. You're loving, but it's not helping. It's actually hurting. They become dependent. You want to guide, direct and help all you can, but you don't want to take away their independence.

I didn't have too much in the way of material things to give my children, so having too much wasn't that much of a problem. But I didn't want them to end up being dependent on others, systems or programs either. The only dependence I wanted my loved ones to have was dependence on God, and I wanted them to have Jesus in their hearts.

–JW

Jesus summarized the Ten Commandments in two directives: love God and love people. Love God is first—this makes it so we can't emphasize the second commandment over the first and get away with it. If we reverse the order, our neighbor becomes an idol, and God will have none of those before Him.

If the poet were trying to say that all we have to do to be approved by God is love our fellow man, he'd be contradicting Scripture. Who is God in flesh? Jesus! According to the first commandment, whom must we love to love God the way He wants to be loved? Jesus! We must never take Jesus out of the equation.

However, if the poet is saying that we can determine how much we love God by how much we love people, then he got it right. Jesus asked Peter three times, "Do you love me?"

Peter said, the equivalent of "Yes" each time.

Three times Jesus told him what that kind of love ought to look like when he said, "Take care of my sheep."[1]

If we don't love people, how can we love God? Indeed, we are to love God and to love people, but we must not love people more than we love God. These are important concepts. God made sure Coach got them right. Take a moment to ponder these thoughts. He wants you to get it right, too.

—JC

Oh, God, deepen my love for You and Your people.
Show me how to tend to Your sheep.
In Jesus' name, I pray.

Spoiled Rotten

Brothers and sisters, we urge you to warn those who are lazy.
Encourage those who are timid. Take tender care of those who are weak.
Be patient with everyone.

1 THESSALONIANS 5:14

The worst thing you can do for the ones you love are the things they could and should do for themselves. I think Lincoln said that first—I'm not sure—but I've used it so much over the years that the saying has become a part of me. I've used it a lot because I deeply believe it.

I'm convinced we do too much for others, and I think it has hurt our nation. I know it has hurt our society and our families. When you do too much, neither countries nor people appreciate it. If people are hungry, give them fish. But after they have eaten, teach them how to fish. Don't keep giving them fish. That makes them dependent on you for their food. It's never good to take away anyone's independence.

I coached my players not to expect time-outs during games, and I didn't want them looking over at the bench for directions. Once the game started, I didn't want them to need me.

Coaches tend to do too much for their players. We get summer jobs for them, so they don't learn how to get jobs. We give them too much help with their studies, so they don't learn how to learn. If we directed them in how to do things rather than doing things for them, they would be a lot better off.

It's the same with our children. We tend to spoil them by overindulging. You're loving, but it's not helping. It's actually hurting. They become dependent. You want to guide, direct and help all you can, but you don't want to take away their independence.

I didn't have too much in the way of material things to give my children, so having too much wasn't that much of a problem. But I didn't want them to end up being dependent on others, systems or programs either. The only dependence I wanted my loved ones to have was dependence on God, and I wanted them to have Jesus in their hearts.

–JW

Needy people can't support themselves, so they need help. People to whom ministry occurs need the people doing the ministry, so we should help to provide for ministers, too. There is also a biblical base for supporting missionaries. For everyone else, 2 Thessalonians 3:10 is clear: "Whoever does not work should not eat." In other words, don't spoil folks by giving them too much of what they haven't got coming. The sons of Eli and David's son Absalom are great examples of what happens when someone is spoiled rotten.

Samuel was given to Eli the priest to be raised for God's service. Eli had two sons that he refused to discipline. In 1 Samuel 3:11-14, God told Samuel to tell Eli that he was going to lower the boom on Eli's spoiled kids: "I am about to do a shocking thing in Israel. I am going to carry out all my threats against Eli and his family. I have warned him continually that judgment is coming for his family, because his sons are blaspheming God and he hasn't disciplined them. So I have vowed that the sins of Eli and his sons will never be forgiven by sacrifices or offerings."

Jumping ahead a few verses to 1 Samuel 3:18, we read, "So Samuel told Eli everything; he didn't hold anything back, 'It is the LORD's will,' Eli replied. 'Let him do what he thinks best.'" Eli was a lousy dad, but at least he took the consequences of his sin like a man.

Absalom was a self-centered piece of work. Apparently he was a hunk, at least according to 2 Samuel 14:25: "Now no one in Israel was as handsome as Absalom. From head to foot, he was the perfect specimen of a man." The Bible reveals that he had some great hair, too. David spoiled him rotten, so the same thing happened to Absalom. He died a violent death but not until David and the nation of Israel went through way too much grief. Spoiling kids has a rippling effect.

Don't play favorites and spoil anyone. The consequences are too great. Take care of needy people because they can't work enough to take care of themselves. Take care of your ministers and missionaries because they are working when they present the good news. But don't give anyone too much. And don't give anything to those who can work but won't.

–JC

Heavenly Father, give me a passion for those who need help but who can't help themselves, give me the courage to keep from spoiling those whom I love, and give me the wisdom to tell the difference. Thank You. Amen.

TODAY'S READING: 2 THESSALONIANS 3:6-15;
1 THESSALONIANS 4:11-12; 5:14; PROVERBS 6:1-5; 1 SAMUEL 3:10-18; 4:5-11;
2 SAMUEL 14:25; 2 SAMUEL 3—15 (FOR THE WHOLE STORY OF ABSALOM)

Doing What Is Right

Then Jesus said to his critics, "I have a question for you.
Is it legal to do good deeds on the Sabbath, or is it a day for doing harm?
Is this a day to save life or to destroy it?"

LUKE 6:9

The National Collegiate Athletic Association (NCAA) has lots of rules. Some of them regulate what a coach can and cannot do for a player. I believed in, understood and always tried to stay within the NCAA guidelines, even though I did not agree with all of them. However, there was a time when I intentionally broke one.

One of my players had received a large number of traffic and parking tickets. Evidently he did not pay them off. Therefore, the police picked him up and threw him in jail on a Saturday night. I was called and I went down to the jail. There were a lot of drunks and people who were different—I wasn't going to leave this young man in there over that weekend—so I bailed him out. Technically that was against the rules. If the NCAA had come down on me, I would not have hidden what I had done, but I would have fought for the right to do it. I had to do what I believed was best for the boy.

After I bailed the player out, I told him that what I was doing violated the rules and that he would have to pay back the amount I had spent. I actually didn't expect him to repay the debt—perhaps by saying what I did I was trying to soothe my conscience. However, if faced with the same situation again, I would do it the same way. The well-being of the boy was more important to me than keeping the rule or the possibility of suffering the consequences.

—JW

In the days the Bible was written, landowners would not harvest the edges and corners of their fields, so the poor would have something to eat. That also was the practice when Jesus walked through a wheat field one Sabbath day.

The Ten Commandments prohibited working on that holy day, but God never intended to forbid eating, healing or doing what's right on the Sabbath. However, the superspiritual religious power brokers of the day (Pharisees, Sadducees, scribes and others) had added almost six hundred man-made rules in an attempt to define what God meant. It was just another way to make themselves out to be like God. Attempting to interpret is one thing, but adding to God's Word is quite another.

Jesus was hungry and violated the man-made rules by grabbing a handful of grain, rubbing the husks off and eating. The Pharisees said, "You shouldn't be doing that! It's against the law to work by harvesting grain on the Sabbath." Remember, Jesus was harvesting to eat it, not sell it—therefore, it wasn't work.

Jesus ticked them off when He reminded them that King David had done the same for his men. If it was okay for David, it was certainly okay for Jesus. Then he added, "I, the Son of Man, am master even of the Sabbath."[1] He intentionally fueled the fire because the master of the Sabbath would be God, and with that statement, Jesus claimed to be God.

On another Sabbath day, Jesus was in the synagogue and noticed a man with a deformed right hand. The Bible records, "The Pharisees watched closely to see whether Jesus would heal the man on the Sabbath, because they were eager to find some legal charge to bring against him."[2] They expected Him to heal the guy. Did you get that? Expected! They not only knew He could do it, but they also expected it. They were more interested in keeping their rules than seeing God at work. So Jesus asks the crowd if it's better to do what's right or keep the rules. He answered when He healed the guy.

The Bible is our ultimate authority. When rules are made that violate it, break those rules. Always do what's right when the man-made rule is wrong, but be prepared, as Coach was, to suffer the consequences.

–*JC*

Father, give me the courage to always do what's right.
And give me the strength to stand up for
the weak and powerless. Amen.

TODAY'S READING: LUKE 6:1-10; MATTHEW 12:9-14; 1 SAMUEL 21:6

No Fear

Work hard for sin your whole life and your pension is death. But God's gift is real life, eternal life, delivered by Jesus, our Master.

ROMANS 6:23, *THE MESSAGE*

After my wife, Nellie, died, I grieved deeply for a couple of years, during which I really didn't care much whether I lived or died. I was pretty low. There were some people who thought I might even do something crazy, but I never considered taking my own life.

I've had concerns about heaven and hell in the past. I don't think about it now. It's a settled matter. I know the promise of heaven God has given each of us. The future, after death, does not scare me.

I was speaking at an event and when I finished my remarks, someone asked, "Coach, are you afraid to die?"

That's an odd question to ask a man over ninety years of age, I thought. "No, I don't think I am," I replied. "I'm not going to intentionally hurry it up, but you know, I'm over ninety years of age. I've had a long life. I have a wonderful family and the Lord has let them all be near me. They're never far away. I had fifty-three wonderful years with Nellie. I've been blessed in so many ways with so many friends. No, I'm not afraid to die. Out yonder somewhere, I'll be with Nellie again, but when? Not until after death. But I'm ready."

–JW

In November 2001 my dad contracted terminal lung cancer. I had always been concerned about his soul, but he wouldn't talk about it. That's why I wrote my book *Playing with Fire*—it was especially for him. I hoped he would read it and accept Christ as his Savior. With the diagnosis of cancer there was no more time to pussyfoot around the issue. I asked him if he had ever read the book like he'd promised. "No, son," he said with very little remorse.

My dad was an earthy kind of a guy, so flex with me while I recount the rest of the story. "Dad, I want you to promise that you'll read my book," I said.

"Okay, junior, it takes me about a half hour every morning to sit on the pot. I'll read a page and use a page."

In early December, I asked him how he was doing with the book. "Well, junior, I had a little bout with diarrhea and I was able to finish it." What a character! I jumped on a plane to Tucson, where he lived.

"You don't have to worry about me and the Lord," he said. "We got it all worked out. I'm right with God."

I pressed the issue, wanting to make sure. "Have you trusted your soul to the care and keeping of the Lord Jesus Christ?"

"Yes, son, I have."

I pressed further. "Dad, have you asked Jesus to be your Savior?"

"Yes, I have."

Three weeks later I held his hand and watched his last breath as he went to be with the Lord. He wasn't afraid.

–GC

God of Heaven, thank You that through Jesus Christ
my Lord I do not have to fear death. Amen.

TODAY'S READING: ROMANS 7:24–8:2; 8:38-39; 1 CORINTHIANS 15:26; COLOSSIANS 1:21-23

Preparation Day

It's impossible to please God apart from faith. And why?
Because anyone who wants to approach God must believe both that he
exists and that he cares enough to respond to those who seek him.

We went to church for as long as I can remember. Every Sunday my mother made sure the family got up and that we were ready to go. She worked harder than any woman I've ever known. My father read to us from the Bible every evening and came as close to living the life of following the Golden Rule as any person I've ever known.

Sunday was a day to honor God and the day when we got together with friends and family. After church, we'd go to someone's house, or people would be at ours. It was the Midwest and this was our way of life.

When I was seventeen, Nellie and I attended the same church. We were both baptized in 1927. I did it because Nellie wanted me to join her. It also pleased my parents.

When I was baptized, I really hadn't accepted Christ. I thought I had, but I hadn't. I wasn't against Christianity, but I knew Jesus wasn't in my heart. I can't tell you when this changed. There was no single event; rather, I gradually came to accept the Master. Around the time my daughter was born in the early 1930s, I knew Christ was in my heart. And I have never doubted it since.

–JW

Coach Wooden was fortunate. He had a girlfriend who was interested in spiritual matters and Christian parents who taught him the value of God's Word, the importance of prayer and the significance of worship. It's interesting that he embraced all three and never wandered, even when he went off to college. He has read the Scriptures regularly since he was a youth, has prayed most mornings and evenings, and has rarely missed going to church. But John Wooden wasn't a believer until shortly after the birth of his daughter in 1934. Prior to that time, Coach wasn't saved. He looked like a Christian and acted like I wish most Christians would act, but he was a cultural Christian. Growing up in the faith and assuming you're a Christian is like being in a doughnut shop and assuming you're a cop. Being there doesn't make you one.

God is always about the *why* of things, not the *what*. God is interested in the heart. And that's why doing the right thing for the wrong reason doesn't cut it with God. Coach was baptized. Right thing! Why? Because he wanted to please his loved ones. Wrong reason! Being baptized for the wrong reason doesn't mean much to God.

I had a similar experience. I was baptized in grade school. I did it because my mom wanted me to do it. She did it because she thought it would be good for me. It didn't do anything for either of us. We both had the wrong reasons. I chose to be baptized again when I was in my early thirties, after I had come back to the Lord—just to be obedient to God. I wanted to get it right.

Baptism was the first ordinance of obedience prescribed by God for believers. God wants us to give our lives to Christ and then, in obedience, identify with His death, burial and resurrection through baptism. In the Early Church, as described in the book of Acts, the first thing new believers did was to be baptized.

Remember: Baptism won't get you saved, but it's the first thing you ought to do after you are.

—JC

Heavenly Father, I want to be obedient to Your Word. I want to identify with the death, burial and resurrection of Your Son. Thank You.

TODAY'S READING: MATTHEW 7:21-23; ACTS 2:37-42; 8:9-13;
ROMANS 6:3-11; PHILIPPIANS 3:8-11

The Big Three

*For all that is in the world, the lust of the flesh and the
lust of the eyes and the boastful pride of life, is not from the Father,
but is from the world.*

1 J O H N   2 : 1 6 ,   *N A S B*

My teams' win/loss ratio had worsened in the two years prior to my worst season as a college coach—a 14-12 finish in the 1959-1960 season. I wasn't sure of the cause. I didn't think it was recruiting, as we were getting our share of quality athletes. I was convinced the difficulty was with my philosophy, but I didn't know where or what. Successful basketball requires intricate attention in three primary areas—conditioning, fundamentals and teamwork. So it was time to make a total analysis of everything we'd done over the years. If my way wasn't the best way, I was certainly open to change.

Failure is not fatal, but failure to change can be.

One way I spotted the changes my teams or I needed to make was to study a portion of the game of basketball each year. For example, one year I read everything I could get my hands on about rebounding. Then I contacted coaches I respected and who knew a great deal about that aspect of the game. I kept intricate records, and I studied my team's rebounding patterns.

As a result of my research, I am one of the few coaches who did not teach a style of rebounding called boxing out. I wanted my boys to get between the opposing player and the ball. I didn't want them to simply keep the man they were defending from getting it. I wanted them to go get it. It worked. We consistently out-rebounded opposing teams, even when my teams had shorter players.

–JW

Some of the seasons of life are spent in a valley, some on a mountaintop. Coach spent time in the valley after his wife died. It was an unavoidable season and was not of his doing. But much of our "valley time" is our own fault. Usually it's sin that drags us down and quenches the Holy Spirit who lives in us. When we do a big sin, we know it. Sins such as adultery, stealing and lying are biggies. We immediately realize that we're guilty.

King David committed adultery and murder. He lived with the guilt for a couple of years and was grumpy the entire time. When he confessed and penned Psalm 51, the greatest prayer of repentance ever written, God forgave him.

Sometimes it is not big sin that has us losing the game of life. There are times when God just feels distant and we're not sure of the cause. All we know is that God didn't move, but we can't figure out what changed.

When that happens, do what Coach did: Analyze the situation. In basketball the problem will be found in conditioning, fundamentals or teamwork. In life we should analyze these big three: lust of the eyes, lust of the flesh and pride of life. The problem always lies within one of those areas.

Ask three questions: Is anything currently more important to me than Jesus Christ? Have I dwelled on immoral thoughts or crossed any line of moral propriety in word or deed? Do I harbor a root of bitterness toward another person?

If God reveals something, stop doing it, make it as right as possible, confess it and enter back into a right relationship with God. Failure is not fatal, but failure to change can be.

–JC

Search me, O God, and know my heart;
test me and know my thoughts. Point out anything in me
that offends You, and lead me along the path
of everlasting life. Amen.

Highest honor: Each year Coach presents the best college basketball player in America with the Wooden Award. In 1977, UCLA's Marques Johnson (top) was the first honoree. The award adorns the mantles of a who's who of college top guns, including the 1987 winner, David Robinson (center), and the 2001 winner, Shane Battier (bottom).

Some of the seasons of life are spent in a valley, some on a mountaintop. Coach spent time in the valley after his wife died. It was an unavoidable season and was not of his doing. But much of our "valley time" is our own fault. Usually it's sin that drags us down and quenches the Holy Spirit who lives in us. When we do a big sin, we know it. Sins such as adultery, stealing and lying are biggies. We immediately realize that we're guilty.

King David committed adultery and murder. He lived with the guilt for a couple of years and was grumpy the entire time. When he confessed and penned Psalm 51, the greatest prayer of repentance ever written, God forgave him.

Sometimes it is not big sin that has us losing the game of life. There are times when God just feels distant and we're not sure of the cause. All we know is that God didn't move, but we can't figure out what changed.

When that happens, do what Coach did: Analyze the situation. In basketball the problem will be found in conditioning, fundamentals or teamwork. In life we should analyze these big three: lust of the eyes, lust of the flesh and pride of life. The problem always lies within one of those areas.

Ask three questions: Is anything currently more important to me than Jesus Christ? Have I dwelled on immoral thoughts or crossed any line of moral propriety in word or deed? Do I harbor a root of bitterness toward another person?

If God reveals something, stop doing it, make it as right as possible, confess it and enter back into a right relationship with God. Failure is not fatal, but failure to change can be.

–JC

Search me, O God, and know my heart;
test me and know my thoughts. Point out anything in me
that offends You, and lead me along the path
of everlasting life. Amen.

TODAY'S READING: GALATIANS 5:17; 6:8; ROMANS 7:15-25; 8:8; PSALM 51:10-13

Highest honor: Each year Coach presents the best college basketball player in America with the Wooden Award. In 1977, UCLA's Marques Johnson (top) was the first honoree. The award adorns the mantles of a who's who of college top guns, including the 1987 winner, David Robinson (center), and the 2001 winner, Shane Battier (bottom).

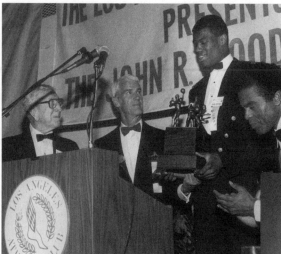

To Coach John Wooden,
The greatest Coach
of all and a wonderful
friend.
love,
Morgan Wootten

To John,
Personal Regards
to a great-great
coach & friend.
Red Auerbach

Time for tributes: At the Naismith Memo-
rial Basketball Hall of Fame, Coach shares a
laugh with all-time winningest NBA coach,
Red Auerbach, and all-time winningest
high school coach, Morgan Wootten (above).
At the White House, Coach accepts the
Presidential Medal of Freedom from
President George W. Bush (center left).
At Pauley Pavilion on the UCLA campus,
Coach thanks the Bruin faithful on Wooden
Day (below).

Making the Right Mistakes

May the Lord bring you into an ever deeper understanding of the love of God and the endurance that comes from Christ.

2 THESSALONIANS 3:5

Jay made a mistake, but I did not mind. When he was on my staff at UCLA, he had the task of developing Lew Alcindor's inside skills when Lew was a freshman. Jay was imaginative in creating drills that kept Lew's attention, but the big man's knees started to get sore. Lew told the trainer, but he did not tell Jay. We had to back off of the jumping drills for a while. Jay's mistake was one of commission, not omission. It was the right kind of mistake to make.

The person who is afraid to risk failure seldom has to face success. I expected my players to make mistakes, as long as they were mistakes of commission. A mistake of commission happens when you are doing what should be done but don't get the results you want, such as anticipating a pass by the opposing player but not actually picking it off.

I didn't want mistakes of omission. That happens when you are not doing something you should be doing, such as failing to cut off the baseline. I would rather have a player try to make a play and fail than be afraid to try.

I wanted my players to be doers. I told them not to be afraid to act. The greatest mistake of all is not taking action when action is needed. The team that makes the most mistakes usually wins, if those mistakes aren't careless.

You can make mistakes and not be a failure if you give it your full effort. Effort includes both preparation and execution. You are never a failure if you gave it your all, unless you blame others for your mistakes. When you place blame, you're making excuses; when you're making excuses, you can't evaluate yourself; and without self-evaluation, failure is inevitable.

You are going to make mistakes. Just make sure you make the right mistakes.

–JW

Coach likes to quote Mother Teresa. She is a great inspiration to him. No wonder. I do not know if she was quick or if she had hops in her younger days, but she certainly was not afraid to take great risks and she never made excuses for her failures.

In 1948, after years of teaching in a convent, Mother Teresa hit the streets of Calcutta. She was there to help the poor, but she too was broke and had to beg. One day a priest angrily rejected her plea. Failure!

Did she run back to the cloistered confines of the convent? No. She became the Slum Sister and attempted to recruit others into what would one day become the Missionaries of Charity. At first, no one responded. "I wonder how long my heart will suffer this," she wrote in her journal. "Tears rolled and rolled. Everyone sees my weakness."[1] Yet onward she went. Mistakes, rejection, weakness and failure did not stop her. Mother Teresa was a doer. By the time of her death in 1997, she had won the Nobel Peace Prize and the hearts of millions around the world. She was a doer who wasn't afraid to make mistakes.

I was discipled in a church with a very strong emphasis on doing. We took the Great Commission literally. The last mandate that Jesus gave was to go into the whole world and make disciples. So we did that. As a church we sent people to other countries and as individuals we told people about Jesus. Some Christians were put off by the way some of us made our presentations. We responded the way Dwight L. Moody once responded to a woman who had criticized his evangelism techniques. Lovingly and often we said, "The evangelism we are doing is better than the evangelism you are not doing. If we are to err, we will err on the side of presenting Jesus. We will not err on the side of not presenting Him." We had decided that the only errors we would make would be errors of commission.

–GC

Heavenly Father, I want to be a doer who
loves You with every fiber of my being. Walk with me
today as I serve You out of a grateful heart.
Help me not to be afraid of making
the right mistakes. Amen.

TODAY'S READING: MATTHEW 22:36-39; 28:19-20; JAMES 1:19-24

Being Quick

So watch your step. Use your head. Make the most of every chance you get. These are desperate times! Don't live carelessly, unthinkingly. Make sure you understand what the Master wants.

EPHESIANS 5:15-17, *THE MESSAGE*

I enjoyed the first of our ten NCAA championships the most, when we won it all with no one taller than six-foot-five. We used a full court press that usually produced one or two surges of six to twelve points each. It worked very well.

People thought we pressed to create turnovers, but that was only a part of the reason. We also wanted to dictate the tempo of the game and cause teams to hurry. That way we could use our quickness. Teams that hurry aren't efficient and don't play their best. It also places a premium on conditioning. We hoped we were in better shape than our opponents were.

Keith Erickson knew how to be quick without hurrying. He initially played the last man back on our press. By the time Keith was a junior, he had learned how to play the position as well as anyone ever has. His instincts and quick jumping ability allowed him to block shots with surprising ease. He had a tremendous sense of anticipation and rarely gave up lay-ins. Opponents usually rushed their shot against Keith, and as a result, they seldom got the shot they wanted or expected; they also usually got only one shot each trip down the court, as he usually got the rebound when they missed. Keith knew how to make opponents hurry with his quickness, while rarely hurrying himself.

–JW

Be quick, but don't hurry. Easy to say, harder to do. Yet it is a lesson that clearly transfers from basketball to life in general.

We want to go at maximum speed but be under control. We seek to be on the edge but not over it. We must be focused but not rushed. We don't want to suffer from the paralysis of analysis but neither do we want to shoot from the hip. Pushing to become all we are capable of becoming without making the same mistake a second time—that's what it means to be quick but not hurry.

People who win at life know God intimately, and they know He only wants a few things from them. God wants us to do everything to His glory by being efficient with all that He's given to us. We can best do that by applying today's principle: Be quick, but don't hurry.

First Corinthians 10:31 shows us that God gets the glory when we become all we can become while dedicating everything we do to Him. When He is the reason for our passion, it pleases our heavenly Father when we are quick but limit our sins. Just be careful about hurrying. It causes turnovers in basketball and results in sin in life.

Our task is to stretch ourselves to become the best we can become at doing the most good with what we have been given and to do it for the glory of God. To do that we have to learn to be quick but not hurry.

–GC

*Heavenly Father, teach me to put Your glory
before my own, help me to become everything
You want me to be, and guide me in the use
of the resources You have given me that I might be
pleasing in Your sight every moment
of this and every day. Amen.*

TODAY'S READING: 1 CORINTHIANS 10:31; MATTHEW 25:15-28; COLOSSIANS 3:12-17

Die Living

For to me, living is for Christ, and dying is even better. Yet if I live, that means fruitful service for Christ. I really don't know which is better. I'm torn between two desires: Sometimes I want to live, and sometimes I long to go and be with Christ. That would be far better for me, but it is better for you that I live.

PHILIPPIANS 1:21-24

I have already noted that the two years after Nellie died were very difficult for me. I would never take my life, but I certainly didn't care if I lived or died during my time of grief and recovery. The poem "Walk Slowly" by Adelaide Love became meaningful during that time:

If you should go before me, dear, walk slowly
Down the ways of death, well-worn and wide,
For I would want to overtake you quickly
And seek the journey's ending by your side

I would be so forlorn not to descry you
Down some shining high road when I came;
Walk slowly, dear, and often look behind you
And pause to hear if someone calls your name.

I still miss Nellie terribly, but all of my family lives within fifty-five miles of me, and many of my former players, whom I consider family, stay in touch with me. I am blessed.

Words often attributed to the philosopher Horace Kellan sum up where I am now in my life:

There are those who guide their lives by the fear of death.
There are those who guide their lives by the joy of life.
The former live dying; the latter die living.
 When I die, I intend to die living.[1]

–JW

Too often funerals are sad. There seems to be no hope. The service is for someone who has died dead. By this, I mean that the focus is on the fact that the person's body no longer has life. He or she is gone from this world.

Memorial services are often sad, too—but they do not have to be. A memorial keeps the remembrance of something alive.[2] There should be hope and assurance. Another way of looking at it is that a memorial service should be for someone who dies living. Think about it: If we really loved the departed and if we know he or she is in heaven, shouldn't we be happy for him or her? Of course! Yet we can still be sad for ourselves, grieving our loss. I think it's possible to grieve for ourselves and still be happy for someone else.

Small-group conversation starters sometimes include a question something like this: What words would you want on your gravestone? I've thought about it some. "Great Dad!" "Wonderful Husband!" "Loved God!" "Finished Well!" "A Man of the Word!" I want all those sentiments to be true of me, but mostly I'd like to reassure my loved ones, so I'd opt for "Died Living." I want people to know that I was born again.

Look at a typical gravestone. Born—Died. A line separates two words and two dates. Life is represented by the line. Where is the hope in that? Born—Died. A dash is not enough. We need more information. If we add another date, another line and three words, the problem is solved. Born—Born Again—Died Living.

With three dates we would know all we needed to know. If the person had been born again, he or she has the certainty of eternity; and if we are born again, too, we have forever to find out what happened between the dates.

We all have a choice. Don't die dead. Choose to die living.

—JC

Heavenly Father, I don't want the words
"born again" to be a cliché in my life.
I want to know Your Son
intimately. May it be.

Getting Even

If you forgive those who sin against you,
your heavenly Father will forgive you.

MATTHEW 6:14

Time spent getting even would be better spent getting ahead. We can't reach our potential when we lose efficiency. When we try to get even, we lose focus on what's at hand and we fail to do the things we need to do to accomplish our task. Thinking about getting even takes our minds off our objectives.

Harboring thoughts of revenge is a bad thing. Forgiveness is much better. We can choose to forgive. When we do that, it sets us free. Mother Teresa exemplified this powerful statement, both in her words and in her life.

I think prejudice and resentment affect us adversely in so many ways. But we must learn from the past, not live in the past. Wanting to get even keeps us in the past. It's a waste of time. Learn and move forward. If success is becoming all you are capable of becoming, harboring resentment and trying to get even will keep you from becoming successful.

One time in high school I was playing against a dirty player. He was trying to get me kicked out of the game. My coach called a time-out and said, "Johnny, they are complimenting you by playing you that way. I want you to take it, and then after we've beaten them, we'll both go over to their dressing room and I'll whip the coach and you can whip the player." We never whipped anyone, and my coach never intended that we would, but I understood what he was saying. He wanted to make sure I didn't retaliate during the game because I would lose focus on the more important targets of staying in the game, playing well and winning.

Most often, officials catch the second hit. If I had retaliated during the game and been caught, I could have been ejected—a result that would have hurt the entire team and our chance of reaching our goal.

–JW

In Bible times it was possible to ransom people out of jail. So the jailers tortured the inmates, knowing that if they did so, the prisoner's loved ones would raise the ransom faster. It was an effective way for the guards to make a few dollars on the side. It was a terrible thing to be turned over to the jailers or, as the *King James Version* of the Bible calls them, "the tormentors."[1]

The Bible describes a ridiculously rich guy with a servant who had borrowed a huge sum of money from him. When the rich man asked for his bucks back, the servant groveled, sniveled and whined, so the rich man forgave the entire debt. What a guy!

That's not the end of the story. There was another man who owed the same servant a puny, piddling amount of money. When the servant asked for his bucks back, the man groveled, sniveled and whined, yet the servant wouldn't budge. He refused to forgive the debt, and he treated his debtor harshly. When the rich man heard about the servant's conduct, Mr. Bigbucks turned the servant over to the tormentors (the jailers). The one who had been forgiven much refused to forgive a little and the consequences were severe.

Through Jesus, God has forgiven all our sin. We're like the servant who was forgiven the huge debt. But when people wrong us and when we refuse to forgive them, the consequences are severe. We are turned over to the tormentors. We have to grant forgiveness to experience the peace God offers.

Forgiveness is giving up your right to get even; it means turning the person over to God. That's all you have to do. You don't even have to trust the person. That takes time. But forgiveness can be done in a moment. Your decision may have to be reinforced periodically when memories bring incidents to mind, but you could start right now by letting go.

–JC

Heavenly Father, You know the resentment
I've been carrying and You know the people toward
whom I carry a deep root of bitterness.
Lord, with each of them I give up my right
to get even. You do what's best for them.
I pray in Jesus' name. Amen.

TODAY'S READING: MATTHEW 18:23-35; 6:7-15; COLOSSIANS 3:12-13

Amazing Grace

God saved you by his special favor when you believed. And you can't take credit for this; it is a gift from God. Salvation is not a reward for the good things we have done, so none of us can boast about it.

EPHESIANS 2:8-9

The first church Nellie and I attended after moving to Southern California in 1948 was the First Christian Church in Santa Monica. We were looking for a church home, and when the pastor walked out, we were amazed. He had been a high school classmate of ours in Indiana and had arrived in town only a short time before we had. What are the chances of that happening? We joined and I was a deacon there until the church was condemned due to damage from the Northridge earthquake in 1994.

Since I had to find a new place to worship, I looked closer to home. One day I saw a certain preacher on television. I particularly enjoyed his teaching, and he was the pastor of a church only five miles away from my residence.

Shepherd of the Hills Christian Church has been home ever since. My daughter, Nan, and her husband, Dick, attend there, too. These days they usually pick me up and take me to Sunday services.

I've been a faithful churchgoer all my life. Even so, I've used the often repeated phrase "If I were arrested for being a Christian, I hope there would be enough evidence to convict me." I say this because I know church attendance alone does not make a person a Christian. It takes a personal relationship with our creator, which only comes about through God's grace. Over the years, I have come to better understand this, and today I appreciate it more than ever.

–JW

Coach understands God's grace, but it's not an easy concept to grasp. To see the full picture we need to understand two other words: "justice" and "mercy." Let me illustrate: Coach Wooden didn't punish players by making them run laps, but for the purposes of my point, let's say the penalty for missing curfew is twenty laps. If a player were to come in late and his coach were to ask him if he broke curfew and he says, "Yes," who makes the decision to run? Not the coach. He's just enforcing the rule. The player makes the decision to run when he chooses to break the rules. Justice is the consequence of our decision to be our own God, and it is getting what we deserve. God doesn't send people to hell. Going there is the choice of the one who broke His rules.

Mercy is a bit different. It's not getting all we deserve.

The coach asks, "How many laps have you run?"

"Ten, sir," the panting player replies.

"How many do you have to go?" the coach asks.

The player thinks, *He's not a math major!* but replies, "Ten, sir."

"Sit down, son," the coach says. "I'll get someone else to run the rest of your laps for you."

Mercy is not getting all you deserve.

Grace is very different from justice and mercy. Grace is getting something we don't deserve at all.

"Son, did you break curfew?"

"Yes, sir, I did."

"Well, sit down over there while I run your laps for you."

The rule is set. When God's curfew is broken, twenty laps have to be run, so Jesus said, "I'll run 'em."

What did we do to deserve that? Nothing. We broke curfew.

When we die, we'll either get justice or grace. Mercy is the time between now and then. Mercy is the time God gives us to make our decision about who will run our laps.

—JC

Father in heaven, thank You that I don't have to
worry about qualifying for the kingdom of God based on my merit.
Thank You that Jesus has already run my laps for me and that
I am now secure because of Your amazing grace. Amen.

TODAY'S READING: PROVERBS 21:15; LUKE 1:50; ACTS 15:11; DEUTERONOMY 5:9-10; PSALM 103:17; EPHESIANS 2:8-9

Avoiding Burnout

WOODEN

I strain to reach the end of the race and receive the prize for which God, through Christ Jesus, is calling us up to heaven.

PHILIPPIANS 3:14

The semifinal game of the 1975 Final Four against Louisville was wonderful. We won in overtime and were headed toward another championship. After the buzzer sounded, I shook hands and talked briefly with Denny Crum, the Louisville coach. Then I headed for the dressing room, as was my routine after every game. But something was different. For the first time ever I did not want to meet with reporters. I knew I had to, but at that time, and never before that moment, I thought to myself, *If I'm feeling this way, it's time to get out.* I knew that my coaching career was over, even though I had three years before mandatory retirement.

In the dressing room I talked to my players. I told them how proud I was of them and spoke about our next game when we would be playing for the championship against Kentucky on Monday. "I don't know how we will do, but I think we will do OK," I assured them. "I think we have enough quickness."

Then I added, "But I want you to know, regardless of how it comes out, I never had a group that gave me less trouble. You gave me no trouble on or off the court all year and I'm extremely proud of you. That's a very nice thing to be able to say about the last team I'll ever teach."

Everybody was stunned.

Some people said they knew I was going to retire. There is not one ounce of truth to that. I had no idea I was going to step aside until I started walking off the floor that night. If anyone had asked me prior to the game if I would be coaching the next year, I would have said, "At least two more years and possibly three."

Now that I am retired I do more of what I want to do. That is what retirement is all about.

–JW

Coach would agree that he had a title and position many people would die for. Even twenty-five years after his retirement, other coaches still call the UCLA gig a dream job. Nonetheless, it was work.

Work was not a part of God's original plan. God had intended us to have responsibilities, but He initially did not plan for it to be hard. The whole concept of work is the result of Adam's original sin in the Garden of Eden. Weeds, thistles and thorns the ground will grow—that is how Genesis describes it.[1] In other words, we'll have to work and it won't be easy. I call it the Genesis curse.

Thanks to Adam, a 60/40 relationship with work is about as good as life is going to get on a regular basis. The 60 percent is the energizing stuff of life. The 40 percent is the stuff that takes the starch right out of you. On the up side you'll have 70/30 days and 80/20 moments. What we really want to avoid is 40/60 or worse. If we live with too much of the negative ratio, we will burn out.

Coach loved to plan and teach (the term he substituted for coaching), but more is required of a head coach. A coach has to live with high expectations, do administrative work, deal with the media, discipline players, correspond with zillions of people, make phone calls, recruit, interact with alumni and a lot more. For Coach, those activities began to cost him energy. Even though it was the pinnacle of his career, it was also the right time for Coach Wooden to say good-bye. He was wise enough to see that if he kept going, he risked slipping from 60/40 to 40/60. That is why Coach got out before he burned out.

When I was forty, I began to identify the activities that cost me energy and the ones that gave me energy. Since then I have been about the business of negotiating my life by decreasing the dejuicing stuff while increasing the stuff that turns my crank. That is living life in the 60/40 mode.

Coach had enough sense to renegotiate his life. I've renegotiated mine. Perhaps you should renegotiate yours.[2]

–JC

*Father God, I want to discover how to serve You
in the way You have wired me to serve. Help me to be the best that
I can be with what You have given me. Give me the wisdom to
know if, when and how I should renegotiate my life.
Thank You, Lord. Amen.*

TODAY'S READING: GENESIS 3:14-19; ROMANS 12:3-8; PHILIPPIANS 1:3-11;
EXODUS 35:30—36:1

Up Yonder

God will open wide the gates of heaven for you to enter into the
eternal Kingdom of our Lord and Savior Jesus Christ.

2 PETER 1:11

Swen Nater was one of my players. He played behind Bill Walton during
his UCLA days, and his best years were in pro ball. He was the ABA Rookie
of the Year and later led the NBA in rebounding one year.

Today Swen works for Costco, and as I have previously noted, he writes
poetry as a hobby. He's very good. I'd finished speaking at a Costco event
when someone asked if I was afraid of dying. In response I mentioned that
I was looking forward to seeing my dear wife, Nellie, up yonder when I die.
The following week Swen sent me this poem:

Yonder
Once I was afraid of dying,
Terrified of ever lying,
Petrified of leaving family, home and friends.

Thoughts of absence from my dear ones,
Drew a melancholy tear once,
And a lonely, dreadful fear of when life ends.

But those days are long behind me,
Fear of leaving does not bind me,
And departure does not host a single care.

Peace does comfort as I ponder,
A reunion in the yonder,
With my dearest one who's waiting for me there.

–JW

We can surmise that God doesn't exist and be an atheist, but that's just another way of saying "I'm God." We can go for the New Age movement and believe that we'll go around in life as many times as it takes to get it right. We can reckon that God grades on the curve and hope we're nice enough to make the cut, or we can place our hope in the Christ of the Bible.

God operates by the golden rule: He who has the gold makes the rules. He has all of the gold, so here's His rule: If you don't trust Me, you won't be with Me in eternity.

We can believe the Bible. The Old Testament was written four hundred to fifteen hundred years before the New Testament, yet there are over three hundred prophecies in the Old Testament that were fulfilled in the New Testament. Some of them are very general, but Jesus fulfilled more than sixty specific prophecies. Keep in mind that He had no control over His place, time or manner of birth; His betrayal; the manner of His death; the Jewish people's reactions; the piercing of His hands and feet; or His burial. Yet each prophecy was specifically proclaimed.

There is more. Jesus would be born in Bethlehem, flee to Egypt, be raised in Nazareth, ride into Jerusalem *on a donkey*, be betrayed by a friend *for thirty pieces of silver* and die by a method of execution that had yet to be invented when described. The specifics go on and on.

If any of the events that had been foretold so long before they occurred hadn't happened the way they were prophesied, then a shadow of doubt could be cast over the whole thing. But they happened. What are the odds of them happening by chance? Isn't it more likely that God orchestrated the events?

The Bible has stood the test. If I were a betting man, I would be willing to bet my soul on it. As a matter of fact, I have! Nell Wooden trusted her soul to Jesus. Coach has, too. And one of these days we'll all be up yonder. You can be there, too—if you make the right choice.

−*JC*

Dear God, thank You for preparing a place for
those who trust in Your Word. Help me to live today
in the light of heaven. Amen.

TODAY'S READING: ROMANS 2:7; 8:18; EPHESIANS 1:18; PSALM 16:11;
MATTHEW 25:34; 2 TIMOTHY 4:7-8

Breaking Ties

And further, you will submit to one another out of reverence for Christ.

EPHESIANS 5:21

It would be a dull monotonous world if we all agreed on everything, but we should never be disagreeable just because we disagree. I use this maxim when I'm speaking about marriage. It worked with Nellie and me. But I also found it to be true in my life.

Arguments are easy to start and probably happen too often. When we become argumentative, we tend to lose control. Some people start yelling at each other. In the end, nothing is accomplished. Moreover, if we're not disagreeable, sometimes we'll actually find out that the other person is right.

How did Nellie and I get along so well? One time we had a disagreement. I had to leave the house for a while. When I got home, there was a card on my pillow. On the card Nellie had written: "Don't try to understand me, just love me." It was a lesson I needed to learn.

Usually, we easily worked out our differences—such as how to spend our money—but once there was what seemed like an irresolvable issue. Our greatest disagreement after we were married came when I enlisted to fight in World War II in 1942. Nellie didn't feel that I should go. She thought I would be endangering the family. As a teacher and as a father of two young children, I could have been exempted from the draft, but I felt I had to serve my country. My obligation as a citizen compelled me.

People will always have problems, but I don't think any problem is unmanageable if each side is more considerate of the other. We must not force our feelings onto others, and we must accept the fact that there can be differences. Nellie may not have fully understood my decision to enlist, but she came to accept it—just as I learned the lesson taught on her note and accepted her. In fact, I still have that card today. It is on her pillow on her side of our bed.

–JW

I loved living in Oregon. Mary and I had built a new home with a wonderful view, and our nest was empty. However, twelve years of the gray and the rain were getting to my wife.

The years had validated Mary as a counselor. She was good at it and wanted more training. She chose the marriage and family therapy program at Fuller Theological Seminary. Many years earlier she had sacrificed to get me through school. I was happy to do the same for her. At fifty years of age we moved into a 400-square-foot married-student apartment in inner city Pasadena, California.

When Mary graduated, she didn't want to go back to Oregon. I did. We struggled to find mutuality. Try as we did, we couldn't. We were absolutely deadlocked. Two people who disagree can usually find mutuality if they try hard enough, but occasionally they can't. That was our situation. How do you break a tie? The Bible has the answers.

Ephesians 5:21 shows that we are supposed to submit to one another. Common courtesy and love should solve most problems. But sometimes there are deadlocks. The next verse in Ephesians declares that wives are to submit to their husbands in the Lord, and the verse after that requires husbands to love their wives as Christ loved the Church. How did Jesus love the Church? He died for it. In other words, a husband is supposed to look after his wife's best interests. That might not always be what either of them wants, but before God, he has to do what he believes is best for her.

Since I was traveling over half the time and since Mary was home all the time, it would have been selfish of me to insist upon moving back to Oregon. It was in her best interest to move where she could work in the sun. So we moved to Santa Barbara. It wasn't a bad second choice for me, and it's been a perfect first choice for her. It is now twelve years later, and it is one of the best decisions we ever made.

—GC

Dear Lord, I don't want to be disagreeable
just because I disagree. Help me to remember to strive for
mutuality in relationships instead of pushing for my own way.
I'd like the interests of others to be more important
to me than they have been. Amen.

TODAY'S READING: EPHESIANS 5:21-33; PHILIPPIANS 2:1-11; 1 PETER 3:1-9

The Best of Friends

There was an immediate bond of love between them,
and they became the best of friends.

1 SAMUEL 18:1

You have to work at making friends; you can't take friendship for granted. I think it's a lot like marriage. Friendship is two-sided. Both sides must work at it.

A friend from Indiana remarked, "Johnny, these people in California aren't as friendly as they are back home."

"What do you mean, Bob?" I asked.

He replied, "Well, coming over here this morning I met a lot of people and not a single person spoke to me. That would never have happened back home."

I asked him, "Did you speak to any of them?"

He made me smile with, "Well, no, I didn't know them."

You have to go out of your way to make friends.

I was feeling low after my great-grandson was born with special needs. I got a call from a friend who had a son with similar needs, and he sent me a poem titled "Heaven's Special Child." It was very meaningful. Shortly thereafter, I wrote this:

At times when I am feeling low,
I hear from a friend and then
My worries start to go away
And I am on the mend.

In spite of all that doctors know,
And their studies never end,
The best cure of all when spirits fall
Is a kind note from a friend.

—JW

It all started while playing Ping-Pong. He was the pastor who came by to visit. As we played and talked, a relationship began to blossom. Those early days led to a long and deep friendship. Except for Jesus, I have no better friend than Sam. He is my Paul.

The apostle Paul established churches all over Asia Minor, wrote much of the New Testament and discipled Titus and Timothy. Sam discipled me like Paul did them. He was there when I reluctantly led a person to Christ for the first time. He got in my face when I was in a spiritual funk and wanted to back out of a speaking gig. He blessed me when I moved on.

Sam has always been about producing followers of Christ, not followers of Sam. My man, Sam, has touched close to seventy people just like me. At last count, that's how many folks have entered full-time service for Christ from bumping up against him.

All the attributes of a biblical friend exist between us. We are loyal to each other and we would drop anything if there were a need.[1] There is love between us that is thicker than a blood relationship.[2] We won't allow known sin to exist in each other's lives and we confront one another when necessary.[3] Sam would lay down his life for me with no questions asked, as I would lay down mine for him.[4] We are friends in every sense of the word.

I thank God for acquaintances and for new friends, but there is nothing like an old friend. There is a bond that results from ministering together and sharing the deep waters of life. We have raised our children together. We've dealt with the seasons simultaneously. I've heard it said that if a person collects a handful of dear friends in a lifetime, that person has been richly blessed.

Perhaps you have a lot or don't have that many. Either way, there is another kind of friend who is greater than any earthly friend. Coach has that friend. Praise God, so do I!

–JC

*Father God, thank You for a friend who looks
so much like Jesus. Help me be as good a friend
to Him as He is to me. Amen.*

TODAY'S READING: PROVERBS 17:17; 27:10; 18:24; 27:17; JOHN 15:13

The Savior

Yes, everything else is worthless when compared with the priceless gain of knowing Christ Jesus my Lord. I have discarded everything else, counting it all as garbage, so that I may have Christ.

In *They Call Me Coach*, I paraphrased words I once heard from someone else that express my thoughts about the Savior:

> I always tried to make it clear that basketball is not the ultimate. It is of small importance in comparison to the total life we live. There is only one kind of a life that truly succeeds, and that is the one that places faith in the hands of the Savior. Until that is done, we are on an aimless course that runs in circles and goes nowhere. Material possessions, winning scores and great reputations are meaningless in the eyes of the Lord, because He knows what we really are and what we really can be, and that is all that really matters.[1]

In this final reading, I'd like to share with you a poem I wrote that sums up why I joined with Jay Carty to write this book:

Need One Know Why
Need one know why we're here on earth?
Does wealth or station prove one's worth?
Is stature gained in three score plus,
A way to measure one of us?

For the answer I must pray,
And it won't matter what I say,
For He to whom I'll speak will know
What is true and what is show.

And His judgment will be fair,
When we are called together there,
Need one know why?

–JW

Coach and I have made the Bible our standard for making life's decisions. The Word of God is crystal clear:

> There is salvation in no one else! There is no other name in all of heaven for people to call on to save them.[2]

Jesus Christ is Lord! He is the Savior.

From the beginning, life has been about who is going to be god. The first rebellion was with Satan. He wanted to set his throne above God's throne.[3] A third of the angelic host followed his lead.[4] Adam and Eve made the mistake of listening to him, too. Today one of the enemy's tactics is relativism. We give ourselves the right to decide what's right and what's wrong, not God. With relativism, we decide our own reality. Sounds like playing God to me.

Sin is the result of rebellion, and rebellion is the result of wanting to be our own god. But playing God doesn't make us God, so whether or not we believe it, if the essence of the Bible is true, then Jesus is the only way to God the Father.

Don't get worked up if you don't agree. Coach loves you and so do I. We're both tolerant. You can believe whatever you want to believe and we will love you just the same. But we love you too much to allow you to risk your soul without saying something. We don't want you to buy into the concept that all faiths reach the same destination and that it doesn't matter what you believe as long as you are a serious seeker. Either that's a lie or Jesus is a liar. Christ made it clear: All faiths aren't the same and it does matter what you believe. One is right and the rest are wrong. We need to discover truth, not self-determine it.

The Bible has withstood two thousand years of scrutiny. It has proved to be truthful on all matters to which it speaks. It is therefore reasonable that its primary thrust must be true. The central theme of the Bible is that Jesus Christ died to reconcile people to God, and Jesus is the only one who possesses the power to do it. He is the Savior. In light of that truth, everything else is meaningless.

–JC

*Heavenly Father, I entrust the care and keeping of my soul
to Jesus Christ my Lord. Amen and amen.*

TODAY'S READING: ISAIAH 14:12-14; PSALM 139:23-24;
MATTHEW 16:24-26; PHILIPPIANS 2:5-11

ENDNOTES

INTRODUCTION
1. Andy Hill and John Wooden, *Be Quick but Don't Hurry* (New York: Simon and Schuster, 2001), p. 56.

DAY 2
1. Satchel Paige, "Satchel Page Quotes," *Satchel Paige: The Official Website*, CMG Worldwide. http://www.cmgww.com/baseball/paige/quote2.html (accessed May 12, 2003).
2. Oliver Wendell Holmes, *Bartleby.com*. http://www.bartleby.com/100/456.44.html (accessed May 12, 2003).

DAY 6
1. 2 Chronicles 1:10.

DAY 8
1. Abraham Lincoln, *Collected Works of Abraham Lincoln*, vol. 4 (Piscataway, NJ: Rutgers University Press, 1953), n.p.
2. Han Suyin [Elizabeth Comber], *Quoteworld.org*. http://www.quoteworld.org/browse.php?thetext=strength,strong&page=22 (accessed June 25, 2003).

DAY 11
1. Source unknown.
2. John Newton, "John Newton's Conversion," *btinternet.com*. http://www.btinternet.com/-gracegospel/newton.htm (accessed May 27, 2003).

DAY 14
1. Source unknown.

DAY 15
1. Source unknown.

DAY 19
1. For more on teaching, see 1 Timothy 3:2; 2 Timothy 2:24-25; 1 Peter 3:15.

DAY 21
1. Helen Steiner Rice, "You Can't Do a Kindness Without a Reward." © 1970 The Helen Steiner Rice™ Foundation—All Rights Reserved. Used by permission of The Helen Steiner Rice™ Foundation, Cincinnati, Ohio.

DAY 22
1. *NASB, KJV, THE MESSAGE*, respectively.

DAY 24
1. Luke 9:61, emphasis added.

DAY 25
1. I wrote a book with John Bradley titled *Discovering Your Natural Talents*. John is a midlife career counselor. He has continued his studies in the areas of knack and wisdom. This material comes from his yet unpublished study of the subject.

DAY 26
1. Philippians 4:13, *NASB*.
2. Ecclesiastes 12:13.

DAY 27
1. Verna Mae Thomas, "The Cross in the Pocket" (St. Louis, MO: Lay Renewal Ministries, n.d.).

DAY 28
1. 1 Chronicles 4:9, *NIV*.

DAY 29
1. Source unknown.

DAY 31
1. See Job 1:21.

DAY 32
1. John Wooden and Jack Tobin, *They Call Me Coach* (New York: McGraw Hill, Contemporary Books, 1988), p. 94.
2. See Matthew 6:33.
3. Hebrews 11:1.
4. See Hebrews 11:6.
5. See James 1:2-4.

DAY 33
1. Matthew 21:23, *NASB*.
2. Matthew 21:31, *NASB*.

DAY 35
1. While this story has been widely repeated, the source is unknown.

DAY 36

1. James 1:2, *KJV*.
2. James 1:2-4.

DAY 39

1. 1 Corinthians 13:4-7.

DAY 40

1. John 16:4.

DAY 41

1. Ann Landers, quoted in *Encyclopedia of 7700 Illustrations*, ed. Paul Lee Tan (Austin, TX: NavPress Software, Wordsearch Corp., 1997), #1641. Used by permission.
2. *Encyclopedia of 7700 Illustrations*, #1642.
3. Ibid., #1662.

DAY 42

1. Sterling Sill, *Encyclopedia of 7700 Illustrations*, ed. Paul Lee Tan (Austin, TX: NavPress Software, Wordsearch Corp., 1997), #3029. Used by permission.
2. Psalm 63:1.

DAY 43

1. Jay Carty, *O. Whillikers in the Hall of Champions* (Ventura, CA: Gospel Light, 2000), pp. 17-19.

DAY 45

1. John 21:15-17.

DAY 47

1. Luke 6:5.
2. Luke 6:7.

DAY 51

1. Mother Teresa, quoted at Navin Chawla, *Mother Teresa* (London: HarperCollins, 1996), quoted at *Sam Wellman's Biography Site*. http://www.heroesofhistory.com/page28.html (accessed June 18, 2003).

DAY 53

1. A variation of this quote is often attributed to the philosopher Horace Kellan.
2. *Merriam-Webster's Collegiate Dictionary*, 10th ed., s.v. "memorial."

DAY 54
1. See Matthew 18:21-35, *KJV*.

DAY 56
1. See Genesis 3:18.
2. For more help with these concepts, see John Bradley, Jay Carty, and Russ Corth, *Discovering Your Natural Talents* (Colorado Springs, CO: NavPress, 1994).

DAY 59
1. See Proverbs 17:17; 27:10.
2 See Proverbs 18:24.
3. See Proverbs 27:17.
4. See John 15:13.

DAY 60
1. John Wooden and Jack Tobin, *They Call Me Coach* (New York: McGraw Hill, Contemporary Books, 1988), p. 95.
2. Acts 4:12.
3. See Isaiah 14:12-14.
4. See Revelation 12:4.

GLOSSARY

We have been basketball people all of our lives and, therefore, tend to talk basketball talk. However, this book is not written just for hoops players and fanatics. In fact, some of you may never have watched a Final Four or heard of a player riding the pine. This glossary is for you. Many of the words have crept into the everyday vernacular of our culture, but taking nothing for granted—and realizing our message of faith is more important than our gab about a game of round ball—we offer these definitions.

Big Ten. A major Midwestern college athletic conference. Purdue University is a member.

Final Four. The semifinals and finals of the NCAA basketball tournament, involving the surviving four teams from all of the playoff brackets.

guard, forward, center. The playing positions on a basketball team. These days the positions are further defined as the point guard, or the "one"; the shooting guard, or the "two"; the small forward, or the "three"; the power forward, or the "four"; and the center, or the "five."

hang time. Time spent in the air when jumping for a shot or rebound.

hops. Jumping ability, as in "He's got great hops."

John R. Wooden Award. An honor given each year by the Los Angeles Athletic Club to the most outstanding college basketball player in the United States (for more information see www.woodenaward.com). Candidates must carry at least a 2.0 grade point average and be advancing toward a degree.

low-post and high-post offense. Post is the position of the center when the offense is initiated. With most of Coach Wooden's teams, he placed his center at the free-throw line (high-post offense). But with Lew Alcindor and Bill Walton, he positioned them at a point closer to the basket (low-post offense).

NAIA. Abbreviation for National Association of Intercollegiate Athletics.

NBA. Abbreviation for National Basketball Association.

NCAA. Abbreviation for National Collegiate Athletic Association.

Pac-Ten (formerly Pac-Eight). A major college athletic conference located on the West Coast. UCLA is a member.

the pine. The bench, which is the place where the players who are not in the game sit.

the ring. An ornate ring that is the prize for winning a championship.

trash talking. Swearing, cussing or insulting another player in an attempt to intimidate or distract.

Wooden Classic. A college basketball tournament played each year in Southern California.

RECOMMENDED READING
OUR FAVORITES

JOHN WOODEN

BOOKS

The Holy Bible

Albom, Mitch, and Stacy Creamer. *Tuesdays with Morrie: An Old Man, a Young Man, and Life's Greatest Lesson*. New York: Broadway Books, 2002.

Douglas, Lloyd Cassel. *Magnificent Obsession*. Cutchogue, NY: Buccaneer Books, 1997.

———. *The Robe*. Boston, MA: Houghton Mifflin Company, 1985.

Dickens, Charles. *A Tale of Two Cities*. New York: Signet Classic, 1999.

Graham, Billy. *Unto the Hills*. Irving, TX: Word Publishing, 1996.

Hunter, James C. *The Servant: A Simple Story About the True Essence of Leadership*. New York: Prima Publishing, 1998.

McCullough, David. *John Adams*. Carmichael, CA: Touchstone Books, 2002.

And almost anything about Abraham Lincoln and Mother Teresa.

POETRY

Bryant, William Cullen. "Thanatopsis."

Coleridge, Samuel Taylor. "The Rime of the Ancient Mariner."

Gray, Sir Thomas. "Elegy Written in a Country Churchyard."

Longfellow, Henry Wadsworth. "Hiawatha's Childhood."

Milton, John. "On His Blindness."

Poe, Edgar Allan. "The Raven."

Tennyson, Alfred, Lord. *Idylls of the King*.

And the poetry of Sir Walter Scott, William Shakespeare and William Wordsworth.

JAY CARTY

BOOKS

God, The Holy Bible

Bell, Martin. *The Way of the Wolf: The Gospel in New Images*. New York: The Seabury Press, 1968.

Boa, Kenneth. *Face to Face: Praying the Scripture for Intimate Worship*. Grand Rapids, MI: Zondervan, 1997.

Buechner, Fredrick. *Telling the Truth: The Gospel as Tragedy, Comedy, and Fairy Tale*. San Francisco, CA: Harper and Row Publishers, 1977.

Colson, Charles W., with Nancy Piercy. *How Now Shall We Live?* Carol Stream, IL: Tyndale House Publishers, 1999.

L'Amour, Louis. *Walking Drum*. New York: Bantam Books, 1985.

Lewis, C. S. *Mere Christianity*. San Francisco, CA: HarperSanFrancisco, 2001.

———. *The Chronicles of Narnia*. San Francisco, CA: HarperCollins, 1994.

McDowell, Josh. *Evidence That Demands a Verdict*. Nashville, TN: Thomas Nelson Publishers, 1999.

Nee, Watchman. *Spiritual Authority*. New York: Christian Fellowship Publishers, 1980.

Richardson, Don. *Eternity in Their Hearts*. Ventura, CA: Regal Books, 1984.

Strobel, Lee. *The Case for Christ*. Grand Rapids, MI: Zondervan, 1998.

Wangerin, Jr., Walter. *The Book of the Dun Cow*. San Francisco, CA: HarperSanFrancisco, 1989.

———. *The Book of Sorrows*. Grand Rapids, MI: Zondervan, 1996.

———. *The Book of God*. Grand Rapids, MI: Zondervan, 1998.

And most of the writings of Tom Clancy and John Grisham.

Kyle Duncan

ABOUT COACH
JOHN WOODEN

These days John Wooden can be found in the stands at UCLA home basketball games and being interviewed on television during the NCAA basketball playoffs. Each spring he presents the Wooden Award for the collegiate basketball player of the year. And many recognize him as the best college basketball coach ever. Off the court, he spends time with his family, former players and an ever-expanding circle of friends.

Into his nineties, Wooden maintains a busy schedule that includes some personal appearances. Somehow he always has time to meet with a high school coach, sign an autograph for a kid or offer a kind word to a fan. In fact, he has such a disciplined regimen that he ably turned around approvals on the edits of the manuscript for this book in half the time authors a third of his age usually take. And, yes, the former English teacher has not lost his skills—ever alert, he caught a few typos!

John Wooden was born on October 14, 1910, in Martinsville, Indiana, the second of four brothers. Coach Wooden's father instilled in his sons the basic principles of honesty, hard work and respect for others. He also passed along to them a love for reading, especially the Bible and poetry.

Wooden was the star of the Martinsville High School basketball team, leading the team to the Indiana state championship in 1927. Two other years his team was the runner-up, and three times Wooden was named to the all-state team. At Purdue University, the five-foot-ten guard was a three-time All-American, but he is most proud of being an Academic All-American. In 1932, he scored about a third of his team's points, led the Boilermakers to the national championship and was named the Helms Athletic Foundation College Basketball Player of the Year.

An English major and academic achievement honoree, Wooden was wooed by New York publishing companies that wanted him to be their Midwestern representative. He, instead, opted for teaching, taking a post at Dayton High School in Kentucky. At Dayton, he coached the basketball and baseball teams for two years. Next stop for the man who would become a basketball legend was Central High School in South Bend, Indiana, where he coached from 1934 to 1943.

World War II interrupted Wooden's basketball career. As an enlistee he served in the United States Navy for three years, achieving the rank of lieutenant. "It was my duty to serve my country," he says without hesitation.

Not long after the Japanese surrendered to General MacArthur and World War II ended, Wooden accepted a post as basketball coach, baseball coach and athletic director at Indiana State University. In two seasons, his Sycamore teams went 47-14 and reached the NAIA finals.

Wooden went west to UCLA in 1948. While his early teams did well, the success of his later teams earned him a place at the top of the all-time list of coaching greats. Over twenty-seven seasons, the Bruins went 620-147 and won a record ten national championships, including seven in a row. Four times his teams went undefeated during an entire season, and at one point, they won a record eighty-eight consecutive games.

Many all-time greats filled the roster on Wooden's UCLA squads. Perhaps the best known are the two centers Lew Alcindor (now Kareem Abdul-Jabbar) and Bill Walton. But there were other All-Americans, including Walt Hazzard, Lucius Allen, Mike Warren, Gail Goodrich, Keith Erickson, Sidney Wicks, Curtis Rowe, Henry Bibby, Keith Wilkes, Richard Washington, Marques Johnson and Dave Meyers.

Wooden retired in 1975, having achieved an unmatched forty-year career winning percentage of over .800, making him one of the winningest coaches ever.

Named NCAA Coach of the Year six times, Wooden has also been honored by *Sports Illustrated* (Sportsman of the Year and 40 for the Ages), the *Sporting News* (Sportsman of the Year) and ESPN (Century's Greatest). In 1961, Wooden was inducted into the Naismith Memorial Basketball Hall of Fame as a player; in 1973 he entered as a coach—one of only two people to ever receive the double honor (Lenny Wilkens is the other). Today, the national college basketball player of the year receives the Wooden Award, presented annually by the Los Angeles Athletic Club.

While many rank Wooden as the greatest sports coach of the twentieth century—his record and acclaim speak for themselves—he considers himself first a teacher. He was obviously peerless as a professor of basketball, but his lessons stretched far beyond the court. He did not consider himself a success unless his students were mentored in physical, mental and emotional disciplines that applied to all aspects of life. As a teacher of life's most important lessons, he excelled, using his Pyramid of Success as a model. He tells his story and expounds upon his principles in several other books including *Practical Modern Basketball*, *They Call Me Coach* (written with Jack Tobin) and *Wooden* (written with Steve Jamison).

On July 23, 2003, President George W. Bush presented Coach Wooden with the highest civilian honor in the United States, the Presidential Medal of Freedom.

Wooden was married to his high school sweetheart, Nell, for fifty-three years. She passed away on March 21, 1985. John and Nell Wooden had two children, James Hugh and Nancy Anne. Today Wooden has seven grandchildren and eleven great-grandchildren. He lives in Encino, California.

At his home, Coach talks with former UCLA coach Steve Lavin.

WOODEN'S STATS AND HONORS

WINNING PERCENTAGE

In 40 seasons of coaching high school and college basketball, Coach Wooden's teams won over 80 percent of their games.

COLLEGE COACHING RECORD

Indiana State   1946-1948   47-14
- 1947 conference title
- 1948 NAIA championship game

UCLA   1948-1975   620-147
- 19 PAC-10 championships
- 10 national championships
- 149-2 record at Pauley Pavilion (UCLA's home court)

UNEQUALED RECORDS AS A COLLEGE COACH

88 consecutive victories	Next best: 60
10 NCAA championships	Next best: 4
7 consecutive NCAA championships	Next best: 2
38 consecutive NCAA tournament victories	Previous record: 13
4 undefeated full seasons	Next best: 1

HONORS AND MILESTONES

- 2003: Presidential Medal of Freedom
- 2000: NCAA, Coach of the Century
- 2000: ESPN, Greatest Coach of the 20th Century
- 1999: *Sports Illustrated* (CNN/SI website), Century's Best College Basketball Coach
- 1999: *Sports Illustrated* (CNN/SI website), Century's Third Top Dynasty of the 20th Century. Wooden's 1964 to 1975 UCLA basketball teams ranked behind only the 1957 to 1969 Boston Celtics professional basketball teams and the 1946 to 1949 Notre Dame college football teams.

- 1997: Published *Wooden*, with Steve Jamison
- 1995: NCAA Theodore Roosevelt Sportsman Award
- 1995: Lexington Theological Seminary Service to Mankind Award
- 1995: Reagan Distinguished American Award
- 1995: Frank G. Wells Disney Award for role model to youth—first to receive it
- 1994: Tom Landry Medal for Inspiration to American Youth
- 1994: *Sports Illustrated* 40 for the Ages
- 1994: GTE All-American Academic Hall of Fame
- 1993: Pathfinder Award to Hoosier with extraordinary service on behalf of American youth
- 1993: CASEY (Citation for Amateur Sports Excellence) Award for exceptional service to amateur athletics—first to receive it
- 1985: Bellarmine Medal of Excellence—first sports figure to receive it; other recipients include Mother Theresa and Walter Kronkite
- 1977: UCLA All-American Marques Johnson named as the first recipient of the John R. Wooden Award
- 1975: California Sports Father of the Year
- 1974: Velvet Covered Brick Award for Christian Leadership—first to receive it
- 1974: California Grandfather of the Year Award, given by the National Father's Day Committee
- 1974: James A. Naismith Peach Basket Award—first to receive it
- 1974: John Bunn Hall of Fame Service Award—first to receive it
- 1973: Whitney Young Urban League Award of Humanitarian Service
- 1973: *Sports Illustrated* Sportsman of the Year
- 1973: Naismith Memorial Basketball Hall of Fame as a coach—at the time, the only Hall of Fame inductee in more than one category
- 1972: Published *They Call Me Coach*, with Jack Tobin
- 1971: Friars Club Coach of the Year
- 1970: *Sporting News* Sportsman of the Year
- 1968: Honored by Christian Church for service and concern for mankind
- 1966: Published *Practical Modern Basketball*
- 1964, 1967, 1968, 1970, 1972, 1973, 1975: College Basketball Coach of the Year
- 1964: Indiana Basketball Hall of Fame, an original inductee
- 1964: California Father of the Year
- 1960: Naismith Memorial Basketball Hall of Fame as a player

- 1943: All-Time All-American Basketball Team, named by the Naismith Memorial Basketball Hall of Fame
- 1932: Big Ten medal for proficiency in scholarship and athletics, given to graduating athlete with outstanding grades
- 1932: Helms Athletic Foundation College Basketball Player of the Year
- 1930, 1931, 1932: All-American basketball player at Purdue University

© ASUCLA

In 1968, Myron Cole presents Coach with the Christian Leadership Award.

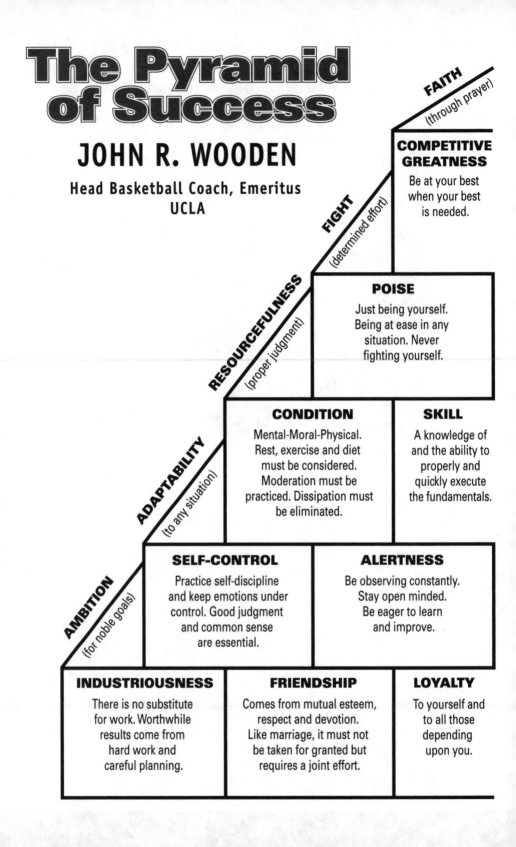

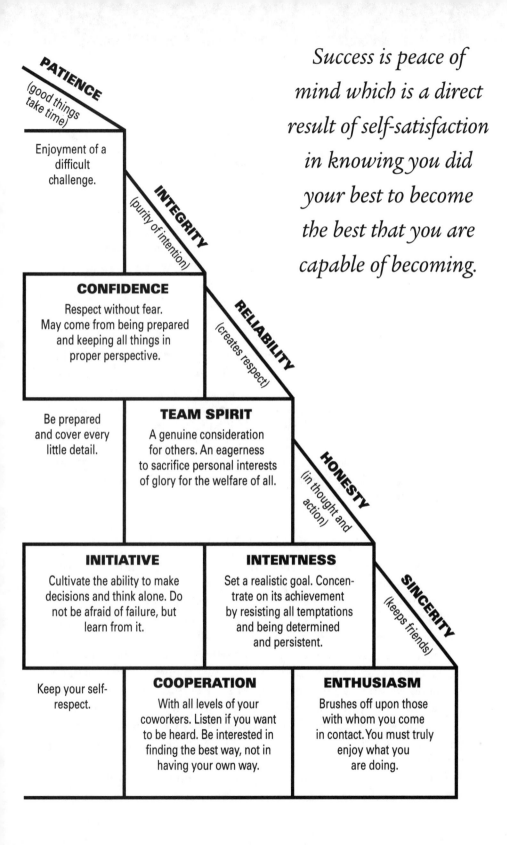

PATIENCE
(good things take time)

Success is peace of mind which is a direct result of self-satisfaction in knowing you did your best to become the best that you are capable of becoming.

Enjoyment of a difficult challenge.

INTEGRITY
(purity of intention)

CONFIDENCE
Respect without fear. May come from being prepared and keeping all things in proper perspective.

RELIABILITY
(creates respect)

Be prepared and cover every little detail.

TEAM SPIRIT
A genuine consideration for others. An eagerness to sacrifice personal interests of glory for the welfare of all.

HONESTY
(in thought and action)

INITIATIVE
Cultivate the ability to make decisions and think alone. Do not be afraid of failure, but learn from it.

INTENTNESS
Set a realistic goal. Concentrate on its achievement by resisting all temptations and being determined and persistent.

SINCERITY
(keeps friends)

Keep your self-respect.

COOPERATION
With all levels of your coworkers. Listen if you want to be heard. Be interested in finding the best way, not in having your own way.

ENTHUSIASM
Brushes off upon those with whom you come in contact. You must truly enjoy what you are doing.

JAY CARTY

I first encountered Coach John Wooden when I was a basketball player for the Oregon State Beavers. In a final-eight game of the 1962 NCAA playoffs, his UCLA Bruins pounded us 88-69. I choked under the pressure and was a nonfactor in the game, so I am sure that I did not impress the man I would later come to know as Coach.

I stood six-feet-eight and weighed 235 pounds. In basketball parlance, I was an inside-outside player. I had enough moves to play close to the basket, yet I was also a pretty good perimeter shooter. I did well enough in college to be drafted in the fifth round by the Saint Louis (now Atlanta) Hawks. The Hawks had drafted three forwards ahead of me, plus they had two all-star starting forwards in Bob Petit and Cliff Hagen—I was realistic enough to see the writing on the wall. I decided to stay in school and finish my undergraduate degree. It's called cramming four years of college into five. I stayed a sixth year to earn a master's degree. During those last two years, I also coached the Oregon State freshman basketball team. Then I went to UCLA to work on a doctorate.

COACH, KAREEM AND ME

A prized recruit from New York also arrived on the Bruin campus that year. At the time, freshmen could not play on the varsity team. That meant the seven-foot-two Ferdinand Lewis Alcindor, Jr. (Kareem Abdul-Jabbar), would play against second-string freshmen in practices and junior college kids in games—at best, the competition would be limited.

Armed with two years of coaching experience, I decided to call Coach Wooden. I offered to do daily workouts with Lew. I thought that my size and background would make me effective. "At least I'd provide more competition than rooks or juco [junior college] kids. That should speed up your kid's development," I reasoned. Coach agreed to give the concept a try. Gary Cunningham was the freshman coach and he graciously allowed me to assist him.

I went one-on-one with Lew for the first thirty minutes of each practice, while the rest of the team went through passing and dribbling exercises. I had to dream up drills that would not bore him. I also worked out against him during scrimmages.

THE SKY HOOK

Lew had patterned his game after Wilt Chamberlain. His primary weapon was a fade-away jumper from the deep left side of the key that took him hopelessly out of rebounding position when he missed. As a staff, we all agreed that when Lew was on the left block, he needed a hook shot across the key and a drop step to the baseline. In nonbasketball jargon, that simply means he needed to expand his game.

I remember telling him, "If you'll develop a hook shot, it will make you five inches taller and your shot will be virtually impossible to block. If you get good at it, then it will end up making you a lot of money." I think he believed me. The sky hook and Lew, aka Kareem Abdul-Jabbar, have become synonymous.

THE BACKBOARD

Lew and I were involved in an incident that changed the game of basketball. Well, that is a bit of a stretch, but it did modify the backboard.

One day while practicing, we simultaneously jumped for a rebound. Another player accidentally pushed both of us and Lew's hand hit the bottom of the backboard. My hand went behind the backboard, up into the screws and supports. Lew jammed a couple of fingers and his thumb. My thumb caught a screw and was bleeding profusely. As Coach came running over, Lew was holding his hand and I had blood dripping off my elbow.

During one of our interviews while preparing this book, Coach smiled as I recounted this story and teased him about going to Lew, standing with him, getting the trainer over to him and making sure he was okay before noticing that I was a bloody mess.

The day after the incident, Coach had someone use duct tape to attach foam rubber around the bottom and sides of all the backboards and around the supports. Some businessmen saw this and patented it, and today every backboard in the country is wrapped in foam. The scar on my thumb reminds me that Lew (now Kareem) and I were the impetus; Lew and I just never got any of the money for foam sales.

THE SCOUT

Coach did very little scouting. We usually played our games back-to-back on Fridays and Saturdays. When we played on Fridays, I would go across town to watch Southern Cal (USC) play the team we would play the following night. I would then brief Coach on Saturday mornings. That's it—just a briefing. There was only one time in the three years I was at UCLA when we fully scouted an opponent—that was the second time we played the University of Houston.

The first Houston game was in the Astrodome, and we played before a huge national television audience. Going into the game, both teams were undefeated—but Lew had double vision from a scratched cornea he'd received the week before. Houston's star, Elvin Hayes, had a superb game and his team won. To this day, he says it was his greatest moment in sports, even though he later became an NBA all-star.

Houston was still undefeated going into the semifinals of the NCAA championship tournament when we faced them for a second time. In preparation for that game, I scouted Houston's last seven outings. My job was to learn its offense and teach it to four of our third-string players—during practice, I was Elvin Hayes.

Talk about a surreal experience! Somehow being Elvin Hayes took the wraps off of Jay Carty. I played the best basketball of my life. I had never shot that well before, and I never played that well again. I only missed eight shots in four days—and I put the ball up every time I got it, because that's what Hayes did. One player was concerned and hollered, "We can't stop him!" Coach calmly replied, "Don't worry. Hayes won't shoot that well." He didn't, and we won easily.

THE LAKERS AND ME

In my third year at UCLA, Coach offered me a full-time position on his staff. By then, however, I knew that coaching wasn't my thing; I loved to play. I was not a good manager of details. Besides, being Elvin Hayes and excelling in those practices had given me enough confidence to try out for the Los Angeles Lakers. At twenty-seven, I made the team and played with Wilt Chamberlain, Elgin Baylor and Jerry West. All three are all-time top-fifty players.

Needless to say, I did not get to play much. My contribution to the team was to sit, drink Gatorade and yell, "Nice rebound," "Way to hustle" or "Great shot." I was usually bloated by halftime.

THE FAST BREAK

The highlight of my career came in the Boston Garden, against the Celtics, back in the days when Bill Russell, John Havlicek and company dominated the NBA.

I was in my usual seat, sipping Gatorade and leading cheers. The second quarter was about to start. The coach, Butch van Breda Kolff, hollered, "Carty!"

I poured a cup of Gatorade and said to the guy next to me, "Pass this down to the coach. He must be thirsty."

"No," van Breda Kolff yelled, "I don't want this. Get your warm-ups off. I want you to play."

I was baffled. It was not even halftime. I never got into games until the final seconds and only then if it was a blowout.

He hollered again, "Get your warm-ups off and get in the game!"

My nickname was Golden Wheels because I couldn't jump and I was slow. My inability to jump is responsible for the saying, There is nothing quicker than white hang time. The Lakers announcer, Chick Hearn, always said that when I ran, it looked like I was treading wood. Since legs are called wheels and since gold is so rare—and I had the rarest legs anyone had ever seen—"Golden Wheels" it was.

I said, "Coach, what do you want me to do?"

The coach was a master strategist. "Carty, you're going to fast-break."

"You're out of your gourd." I was always respectful, but this was crazy.

"Nobody would ever expect it."

I played back in the days when there was a center jump at the start of each quarter. Wilt usually out-jumped Russell.

In the huddle, our coach explained what he wanted us to do. He told me to run toward Boston's hoop as the referee threw the ball up for the tip-off. Wilt would tap it to Elgin, and without looking, Elgin was to hit the ball back toward the Celtics' hoop and me. Since no one would ever expect me to fast-break, I should be able to get the ball and score a layup in Boston Garden.

As I thought about it, I realized the coach was right. Havlicek would not expect me to go. I would get a head start of a couple of steps before he even reacts. Then he will stand and stare at me, doing a double take, because he will not remember ever seeing anyone working that hard going that slow. That should give me a couple more steps head start. Three or four steps are a quarter of a court for me. With only another quarter of a court to go, surely we should at least get to the hoop at the same time. I am three inches taller than Havlicek, so I should be able to score a layup in Boston Garden.

It sounded like a great plan, so I lined up. It was going to be hard to run with my legs shaking. Having never played in Boston Garden before, I was pretty nervous.

As the ref tossed the ball in the air, I took off. Wilt tapped the ball to Elgin and he hit it back, slightly to my side. The plan was working. There was nothing between their hoop and me. All I had to do was dribble three times.

I'm a forward, not a guard. Guards are better ball handlers than forwards. And I'm right handed, not left. I knew that Havlicek would flash from the right side, so I had to dribble the ball with my left hand. A player always wants to keep his body between the ball and the defensive man. I just pushed the ball in front of me and ran to catch up to it, pushed it again and ran to catch up. I could hear Havlicek coming after me and I knew he was close—I could feel his breath on the back of my neck.

As I got to the hoop, I planted my right foot in order to transfer my forward momentum into a stationary position to allow my inertia to carry me skyward. I was going to jump!

Havlicek made a giant mistake. He misjudged my speed. I was going much slower than he thought and he flashed on by. I soared into the air (at least two or three inches) and placed the ball on the glass, an inch and a half too far over to the right. The ball caught the inside lip of the rim and spun in the cylinder, twice. It looked like it might spin out.

I thought, *Please don't miss a layup in Boston Garden on national TV. Please go in. Please!*

It did and I was ecstatic. I was one for one. I had two points. I said to myself, *This game's easy.*

THE ROOKIE OF THE YEAR?

The Celtics missed a shot. We got the rebound and came down on offense. Someone threw me the ball, twenty-three feet from the basket on the left side. I weighed the alternatives. My first option was to pass. There were four of my teammates to pass to, but there were five Celtics in the way. The odds were bad, so I decided not to throw it.

My second option was to dribble. But I wear size fifteen shoes. That's a lot of irregular surface on the floor. What happens when a round ball hits an irregular surface? Who knows? So I didn't dare dribble.

There were only eight seconds left on the twenty-four-second clock (that is how long each side has to shoot the ball). What could I do? Yes! I let one go from twenty feet out.

As the ball left my hand, it went straight, which surprised me. Shots I put up were rarely straight. My shot makes that wonderful swish sound, so now I'm two for two, with four points. I think, *Bonus! Give the kid a bonus. And don't pull me out of the game yet. Let me go some. I'm doing great. I'm bordering on awesome!*

Russell, Havlicek and company went down to their end, shot and missed. We again got the rebound. As our offense began, I was on the right side, nineteen feet out. Somebody threw me the ball. Without hesitating, I said, "In your face! I'm going to do it from nineteen!"

Bingo! I'm three for three. I've got six points and I think, *Rookie of the year! Get it all while you're here!*

THE REBOUND AND THE GATORADE

The Celtics went down, shot and missed. We got another rebound. This time one of my teammates shot. Whoa, was I mad! I wanted the ball! *Give me that ball!* I maneuvered in to be in position to get the rebound and found myself standing next to the great Bill Russell.

The shot missed and bounced straight up. Russell rocketed toward the roof for the rebound. I had never seen anybody jump so high. I turned and stared right into his navel.

But as the ball came down, it hit the front of the rim. Bill hadn't expected that and had mistimed his jump. As he started down, the ball also started down, just above his reach. Using my legs as springs, I again soared into the air (two or three inches) and snatched the rebound.

Russell waited for me to shoot. He stood there with his arms extended upward and his legs coiled, poised, waiting for me to jump, so he could block my shot and tattoo the Spalding insignia across my forehead. But I had already jumped and he didn't know it.

Now I had eight points at Boston Garden! Forget Russell, Havlicek, Chamberlain, West and Baylor—this was Carty time. To this day I don't know exactly what happened. It was as if someone had sucked the last bit of oxygen out of the gym.

I had run, jumped and shot hard. I was exhausted and exhilarated. That is when the Gatorade set in. Remember what I was doing on the bench before the coach had his brilliant idea? Sipping away. Try drinking that much Gatorade and then playing at full throttle. It will not stay down. That's what happened—in Boston Garden on national television. I threw up! It was the highlight of my career.

THE END AND THE NEW BEGINNING

We missed getting the ring by a hoop in the seventh game of the NBA finals, against Russell and those same Celtics, but for one spectacular year I had walked among NBA giants.

Looking back on it, Lew did more for me than I did for him. And I suppose that I should thank Elvin Hayes, too. If it had not been for them, I might not have gotten to play in the NBA.

That summer the Lakers were going to trade me. I didn't want to leave Los Angeles and the base salary was only $15,000 a year (today's players get nearly $300,000), so I decided to retire from the NBA.

The Lakers were adding a color commentator to assist the legendary Chick Hearn with his play-by-play announcing. I auditioned and was offered the job. In those days, in addition to calling the games, I would have had to be the team's traveling secretary, sell season tickets in the off-season and make seventy-five outside speaking appearances. They offered $12,000. I said I would do it for $20,000. They said no, and I passed on the opportunity. Nobody told me that for speaking engagements I would get honorariums that would have amounted to at least $30,000 above the base salary. Had I not been so naïve, I am sure I would have been a successful broadcaster. I had the voice and the knowledge. As it turned out, however, I became a pretty good verbal communicator in a different arena. But it took a few years to get there. I had to come back to God. I'd been away for a long time.

GOD AND ME

During grade school I occasionally went to church with a family down the street; sometimes I went with my mom. One time during an altar call, my mom asked me to go forward with her. She thought it would provide salvation for me. I went because she nudged me. We were even baptized together. We both believed in God. We both believed the Bible. She even gave me one. But neither one of us was born again. Our reasons were not right. We were not interested in a personal relationship with Christ. We wanted to please each other, not our heavenly Father.

Later in life, we would both get it right. My mom prayed to receive Christ when she was sixty-five, some twenty-six years later. My moment came earlier, when I was a sophomore in high school.

During my high school years, home was China Lake, a small town in the high desert in Southern California, ninety miles from Death Valley. It was not exactly hell, but you could see it from there.

THE EYE OPENER

Let's pick up my story when I was six-foot-three. I happened to be fourteen years old at the time and weighed a little less than a hundred and thirty pounds. In those days, a microphone stand and I had a lot in common.

I was hitchhiking—this was back in the 1950s when it was relatively safe. It was a Friday night and a guy picked me up. During the course of the six- or seven-minute ride, he asked if I would go to church with him. I really didn't want to go, but being a conflict avoider, what was I going to do? I said, "Umm, ahh, err, okay."

I was sitting eight rows back on the left side, and the guy who was preaching was a classic fire-and-brimstone man. When he opened his mouth he was talking turn or burn, flip or fry, change your stroke or go down in smoke. When he preached, he didn't just talk; instead, he flung the words at you, in volleys and salvos.

He quoted a Scripture as only he could, screaming, "We've all sinned and come short of the glory of *God!*" [Romans 3:23, emphasis added].

Although I believed him, I thought to myself, *Some more than others. If this guy wants to meet some people who are into sin, I'll introduce him to some of my buddies at school. Some of them actually do the kinds of things I only think about.*

I saw myself as a good kid. I didn't even lie to my folks. Surely none of this applied to me. Then the speaker yelled, "The wages of sin is death, separation from God, hell!"

I thought about that. I knew if someone committed murder, he or she would get the electric chair, life in prison or a lethal injection. If a person robbed a gas station, he or she would get five to ten in the state pen. If anyone lied to his or her parents, he or she might get his or her hand slapped, depending on the mood the parents were in at the time. In other words, there are degrees of punishment to fit the severity of the crime. So when this guy tells me God punishes all sin with just one punishment (hell), I think, *That's not fair*, and was ready to pass on the whole Christian deal.

Then the preacher said, "All sin is the same in God's eyes, because sin is just saying no to God."

I hadn't seen myself as a sinner, but I had broken a few rules and I'd thought about breaking a lot of them. It was then that I realized that indeed I was a sinner, separated from God.

The preacher told me about Christ and my need to invite Jesus into my life. He said that God's Son would do the rest; He would cleanse me, solve my sin problem, reconcile me to God and make me His child. He would do all those things if I would ask Him in. I jumped at the opportunity. Quite frankly, I didn't want to go to hell. I even walked down the aisle to the front of the church for the altar call. Only this time I did it for me.

I believed Christ died for my sins, and I repented of any notion that I could be nice or good enough on my own to stand before God and be okay. I became a legitimate believer, but I quickly turned lukewarm. I got colder in college, and by the time I was playing for the Lakers and when I first got into business, I hardly thought about the Lord.

THE HEART TUGGER

A year after entering the business world, my wife and I started attending church again. It was a last-gasp attempt to save our marriage. On our third Sunday, we were invited to a couple's retreat. That is another story for another book, but the end result was me standing before God again, telling

Him how I had messed up. God didn't flinch. The Father always welcomes His wayward children when they come to their senses. I finally made Jesus the Lord of my life.

THE MINISTRY YEARS

Life moved swiftly after I made that commitment. I spent four years in business and being discipled at my church, and then I went into the ministry, running a Christian Camp. After five years there I worked as a church consultant for Churches Alive. Then I started Yes! Ministries. My motto has been Helping people say yes to God. For more than twenty-five years, I served as a traveling preacher.

In May 2002, I contracted a paralyzed vocal cord and I have not spoken to a group since. For months, I wondered if God had any further use for me. Now I get to write a book with Coach. How great is that!

People occasionally ask if I have a life verse. Being six-foot-eight, I usually say Isaiah 28:20 (*NIV*): "The bed is too short to stretch out on, the blanket too narrow to wrap around you." But that is just for fun. My real life verse has become

> Search me, O God, and know my heart; test me and know my anxious thoughts. See if there is any offensive way in me, and lead me in the way everlasting (Ps. 139:23-24, *NIV*).

Jay and Mary Carty at their home away from home, Hawaii.

ORDER JAY CARTY'S BOOKS, AUDIOCASSETTES AND VIDEOCASSETTES AT JAYCARTY.COM

COUNTERATTACK! TAKING BACK GROUND LOST TO SIN
(BOOK, AUDIOCASSETTE AND VIDEOCASSETTE)

Have your nostrils flared lately? Have you ever had the hots? Have you been chasing the wind? If you answered yes to any of these questions, then you've probably given the devil a foothold in your life. *Counterattack* will teach you how to take back the ground you've lost to the enemy. Learn why your prayers sometimes seem powerless and how you can resist temptation. Find out how to climb out of the swamp and scrape off the leeches of the devil's henchmen. *Counterattack* will either be one of the most serious, fun books you've ever read, or it will be one of the most fun, serious books you've ever read. I'm not sure. One thing is certain: It clearly shows how you can be delivered from the bondage of sin. Includes a study guide.

SOMETHING'S FISHY! GETTING RID OF THE CARP IN YOUR LIFE
(BOOK AND AUDIOCASSETTE)

What do you call the things in life that choke your growth and cloud your view of Christ? The apostle Paul calls them dung. Jay Carty calls them carp. People infested with carp live in a place Jay calls Tweener's Bog, a no-man's-land between commitment and unbelief. They want just enough faith to get to heaven but not enough to change their lives. It's hard to know if they are what they appear to be—do they really have saving faith or are they fooling everyone, including themselves?

PLAYING WITH FIRE: DO NICE PEOPLE REALLY GO TO HELL? (BOOK AND AUDIOCASSETTE)

Apologetics at its contemporary best. At last there is a book you can confidently hand to your friends without them thinking you're preaching at them. Jay wrote this book for his dad, who got saved at the age of eighty-three, after reading this book. Includes a study guide.

DISCOVERING YOUR NATURAL TALENTS (BOOK)

Love what you do and do what you love! This book is coauthored by John Bradley, president of the IDAK group, a natural-talent assessment organization in Portland, Oregon. Together, Jay and John help you discover your God-given abilities and put them to work in every area of your life. Includes a small-group-discussion study guide.

O. WHILLIKERS IN THE HALL OF CHAMPIONS (BOOK AND AUDIOCASSETTE)

Helping young people prepare for life was never more fun! The eight colorfully illustrated stories in this book tell it like it is for today's kids. *O. Whillikers in the Hall of Champions* brings the Beatitudes of Jesus to life by showing how kids who had it tough learned to be godly in spite of their circumstances. Humorous situations and animal characters get both six- to eleven-year-old children and their parents to stop, think and answer the questions at the beginning and end of each story. With each visit to the Hall of Champions, kids grow to love and learn from the adventures of these eight comical characters.

THE SPORTS PAGES (BOOKLET)

This is a compilation of quotes from athletes. There is one for each day of the year.

ONLY TENS GO TO HEAVEN (BOOKLET)

This illustrated booklet contains the plan of salvation.

JAY CARTY
1033 NEWTON ROAD
SANTA BARBARA, CA 93103
805-962-7579
jay@jaycarty.com

Enjoy more of Coach Wooden's value-based books

Inch and Miles: The Journey to Success
By Coach John Wooden
Illustrated by Sue Cornelison

Based upon Coach John Wooden's Pyramid of Success, this long-awaited book delivers a gentle message for children about the personal greatness that lives within them.

Available September 1, 2003
Full-color picturebook • $15.95
Hardcover with dust jacket • 40 pages
ISBN 0-7569-1410-8
Publisher: Perfection Learning
Phone: (800) 831-4190
perfectionlearning.com

"No one better exemplifies the phrase 'character counts' than John Wooden. Whatever he touches is gold and in Inch and Miles Coach Wooden's wisdom and decency are translated into marvelously engaging and instructive life lessons."

Michael Josephson
Josephson Institute of Ethics

Recommended by Campus Crusade for Christ and Athletes in Action.

Wooden: A Lifetime of Observations and Reflections On and Off the Court
By Coach John Wooden with Steve Jamison

Coach John Wooden's best-seller shares the straight and true lessons he has lived his life by; lessons that have been called 'the code of ethics which created America's strength.'

"WOODEN is a winner!"
Reverend Robert Schuller
The Hour of Power
Crystal Cathedral

Hardcover • 240 pages
ISBN: 0-8092-3041-0
Publisher: McGraw-Hill/Contemporary Books

Visit Coach's official Web site: CoachJohnWooden.com

Check Out These Other Best-Sellers

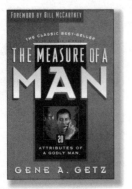

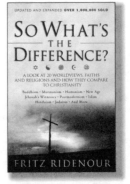